BY ADRIENNE RICH

An Atlas of the Difficult World:
Poems 1988–1991

Time's Power: Poems 1985–1988

Blood, Bread, and Poetry: Selected Prose 1979–1986

Your Native Land, Your Life

The Fact of a Doorframe: Poems Selected and New 1950–1984

Sources

A Wild Patience Has Taken Me This Far

On Lies, Secrets, and Silence: Selected Prose, 1966–1978

The Dream of a Common Language

Twenty-one Love Poems

Of Woman Born; Motherhood As Experience and Institution

Poems: Selected and New, 1950–1974

Diving into the Wreck

The Will to Change

Leaflets

Necessities of Life

Snapshots of a Daughter-in-Law

The Diamond Cutters

A Change of World

COLLECTED

EARLY POEMS

1950–1970

W · W · NORTON & COMPANY

NEW YORK · LONDON

COLLECTED

EARLY POEMS

1950–1970

ADRIENNE RICH

The text of this book is composed in Garamond no. 3
with the display set in Bauer Text Initials.
Composition and manufacturing by
The Maple-Vail Book Manufacturing Group.
Book design by Antonina Krass

Library of Congress Cataloging-in-Publication Data
Rich, Adrienne Cecile.
    [Poems. Selections]
    Collected early poems, 1950–1970 / Adrienne Rich.
        p.   cm.
    Includes index.
    I. Title.
    PS3535.I233A6   1993
    811'.54—dc20   92-13150

ISBN 0-393-03418-6
W.W. Norton & Company, Inc., 500 Fifth Avenue, New York, N.Y. 10110
W.W. Norton & Company Ltd., 10 Coptic Street, London WC1A 1PU
1 2 3 4 5 6 7 8 9 0

CONTENTS

POEMS *(1950–1951)*

THE DIAMOND CUTTERS *(1955)*

SNAPSHOTS OF A DAUGHTER-IN-LAW *(1963)*

POEMS (*1955–1957*)

NECESSITIES OF LIFE (1966)

PART ONE: POEMS 1962–1965

PART TWO: TRANSLATIONS FROM THE DUTCH

POEMS *(1962–1965)*

LEAFLETS *(1 9 6 9)*

PART ONE: NIGHT WATCH

PART TWO: LEAFLETS

PART THREE: GHAZALS (HOMAGE TO GHALIB)

THE WILL TO CHANGE *(1971)*

POEMS *(1969)*

FOREWORD

This edition contains all the poems included in my first six books, from *A Change of World* (1951) to *The Will to Change* (1971). A few previously uncollected poems of this period, which appeared in *The Fact of a Doorframe: Poems Selected and New, 1950–1984,* are also included. I have made no revisions since those few noted in that collection. Notes to the poems are consolidated from all the books.

The one book from which I was tempted to delete poems is *The Diamond Cutters,* my second volume. It received much praise; but too many of the poems were, at best, facile and ungrounded imitations of other poets—Elinor Wylie, Robert Frost, Elizabeth Bishop, Dylan Thomas, Wallace Stevens, Yeats, even English Georgian poets—exercises in style. I have let them stand, however, rather than deny what I then saw fit to publish. Many of the poems in *The Diamond Cutters* seem to me now a last-ditch effort to block, with assimilation and technique, the undervoice of my own poetry. With the poems in *Snapshots of a Daughter-in-Law* (1963), I began trying, to the best of my ability, to face the hard questions of poetry and experience.

The word "change" occurs in the titles of both the first and last books in this collection and in the first and the last poems. "Storm Warnings" is a poem about powerlessness—about a force so much greater than our human powers that while it can be measured and even predicted, it is beyond human control. All "we" can do is create an interior space against the storm, an enclave of self-protection, though the winds of change still penetrate keyholes and "unsealed apertures."

Nothing in the scene of this poem suggests that it was written in the early days of the Cold War, within a twenty year old's earshot of World War II, at the end of the decade of the Warsaw Ghetto and Auschwitz, Hiroshima and Nagasaki, in a climate of public fatalism about World War III. The poet assumes that change is to be averted if it can be, defended against if it must come. (An enormous military-industrial complex, now inextricable from government, was even then being erected in the name of "defense." The Left was beleaguered and in tatters; the new wave of the African-American movement toward full citizenship had not yet begun.) "Change" here means unpredictability, unrest, menace—not something "we" might desire and even help bring to pass.

My generation of North Americans had learned, at sixteen, about the death camps and the possibility of total human self-extinction through nuclear war. Still, at twenty, I implicitly dissociated poetry from politics. At college in the late 1940s, I sat in classes with World War II vets on the G.I. Bill of Rights; I knew women who campaigned for Henry Wallace's Progressive party, picketed a local garment factory, founded a college NAACP chapter, were recent refugees from Nazism. I had no political ideas of my own, only the era's vague and hallucinatory anti-Communism and the encroaching privatism of the 1950s. Drenched in invisible assumptions of my class and race, unable to fathom the pervasive ideology of gender, I felt "politics" as distant, vaguely sinister, the province of powerful older men or of people I saw as fanatics. It was in poetry that I sought a grasp on the world and on interior events, "ideas of order," even power.

I was like someone walking through a fogged-in city, compelled on an errand she cannot describe, carrying maps she cannot use except in neighborhoods already familiar. But the errand lies outside those neighborhoods. I was someone holding one end of a powerful connector, useless without the other end. Elsewhere, I have tried to describe some of the forces that catalyzed these poems as they catalyzed the life I was living over those twenty years.*

I began dating poems in 1954. I had come to the end of the kind of poetry I had collected in *The Diamond Cutters* and felt embarked

---

*See "When We Dead Awaken: Writing As Re-Vision" in *On Lies, Secrets and Silence* (1979) and "Blood, Bread, and Poetry: The Location of the Poet" in *Blood, Bread, and Poetry* (1986).

on a process that was precarious and exploratory; I needed to allow the poems to acknowledge their moment. From *Snapshots of a Daughter-in-Law* on, as far as possible (some poems having been written over two or three years), I have arranged my books in chronological order as the poems were written. For my first two books, I cannot remember chronology; I do know that "Storm Warnings" was written in 1949, "Tear Gas," the last poem in this collection (uncollected until *The Fact of a Doorframe*), in 1969. But some of the poems in *A Change of World* were written as early as 1947–1948, and the last few poems in *The Will to Change* in 1970. I have therefore settled on 1950–1970 as the essential time frame for *Collected Early Poems*.

A CHANGE OF

WORLD

(1 9 5 1)

For Theodore Morrison

STORM WARNINGS

The glass has been falling all the afternoon,
And knowing better than the instrument
What winds are walking overhead, what zone
Of gray unrest is moving across the land,
I leave the book upon a pillowed chair
And walk from window to closed window, watching
Boughs strain against the sky

And think again, as often when the air
Moves inward toward a silent core of waiting,
How with a single purpose time has traveled
By secret currents of the undiscerned
Into this polar realm. Weather abroad
And weather in the heart alike come on
Regardless of prediction.

Between foreseeing and averting change
Lies all the mastery of elements
Which clocks and weatherglasses cannot alter.
Time in the hand is not control of time,
Nor shattered fragments of an instrument
A proof against the wind; the wind will rise,
We can only close the shutters.

I draw the curtains as the sky goes black
And set a match to candles sheathed in glass
Against the keyhole draught, the insistent whine
Of weather through the unsealed aperture.
This is our sole defense against the season;
These are the things that we have learned to do
Who live in troubled regions.

AUNT JENNIFER'S TIGERS

Aunt Jennifer's tigers prance across a screen,
Bright topaz denizens of a world of green.
They do not fear the men beneath the tree;
They pace in sleek chivalric certainty.

Aunt Jennifer's fingers fluttering through her wool
Find even the ivory needle hard to pull.
The massive weight of Uncle's wedding band
Sits heavily upon Aunt Jennifer's hand.

When Aunt is dead, her terrified hands will lie
Still ringed with ordeals she was mastered by.
The tigers in the panel that she made
Will go on prancing, proud and unafraid.

VERTIGO

As for me, I distrust the commonplace;
Demand and am receiving marvels, signs,
Miracles wrought in air, acted in space
After imagination's own designs.
The lion and the tiger pace this way
As often as I call; the flight of wings
Surprises empty air, while out of clay
The golden-gourded vine unwatered springs.
I have inhaled impossibility,
And walk at such an angle, all the stars
Have hung their carnival chains of light for me:
There is a streetcar runs from here to Mars.
I shall be seeing you, my darling, there,
Or at the burning bush in Harvard Square.

THE ULTIMATE ACT

What if the world's corruption nears,
The consequence they dare not name?
We shall but realize our fears
And having tasted them go on,
Neither from hope of grace nor fame,
Delivered from remorse and shame,
And do the things left to be done
For no sake other than their own.
The quarry shall be stalked and won,
The bed invaded, and the game
Played till the roof comes tumbling down
And win or lose are all the same.
Action at such a pitch shall flame
Only beneath a final sun.

WHAT GHOSTS CAN SAY

When Harry Wylie saw his father's ghost,
As bearded and immense as once in life,
Bending above his bed long after midnight,
He screamed and gripped the corner of the pillow
Till aunts came hurrying white in dressing gowns
To say it was a dream. He knew they lied.
The smell of his father's leather riding crop
And stale tobacco stayed to prove it to him.
Why should there stay such tokens of a ghost
If not to prove it came on serious business?
His father always had meant serious business,
But never so wholly in his look and gesture
As when he beat the boy's uncovered thighs
Calmly and resolutely, at an hour
When Harry never had been awake before.
The man who could choose that single hour of night
Had in him the ingredients of a ghost;
Mortality would quail at such a man.

An older Harry lost his childish notion
And only sometimes wondered if events
Could echo thus long after in a dream.
If so, it surely meant they had a meaning.
But why the actual punishment had fallen,
For what offense of boyhood, he could try
For years and not unearth. What ghosts can say—
Even the ghosts of fathers—comes obscurely.
What if the terror stays without the meaning?

THE KURSAAL AT INTERLAKEN

Here among tables lit with bottled tapers
The violins are tuning for the evening
Against the measured *"Faites vos jeux,"* the murmur,
Rising and falling, from the gaming rooms.
The waiters skim beneath the ornate rafters
Where lanterns swing like tissue-paper bubbles.
The tables fill, the bottled candles drip,
The gaming wheels spin in the long salon,
And operetta waltzes gild the air
With the capricious lilt of costume music.

You will perhaps make love to me this evening,
Dancing among the circular green tables
Or where the clockwork tinkle of the fountain
Sounds in the garden's primly pebbled arbors.
Reality is no stronger than a waltz,
A painted lake stippled with boats and swans,
A glass of gold-brown beer, a phrase in German
Or French, or any language but our own.
Reality would call us less than friends,
And therefore more adept at making love.

What is the world, the violins seem to say,
But windows full of bears and music boxes,
Chocolate gnomes and water-color mountains,
And calendars of French and German days—
Sonntag and *vendredi,* unreal dimensions,
Days where we speak all languages but our own?
So in this evening of a mythical summer
We shall believe all flowers are edelweiss,
All bears hand-carved, all kisses out of time,
Caught in the spinning vertigo of a waltz.

The fringe of foam clings lacelike to your glass,
And now that midnight draws with Swiss perfection
The clock's two hands into a single gesture,
Shall we pursue this mood into the night,
Play this charade out in the silver street
Where moonlight pours a theme by Berlioz?
If far from breath of ours, indifferent, frozen,
The mountain like a sword against the night
Catches a colder silver, draws our sight,
What is she but a local tour de force?

The air is bright with after-images.
The lanterns and the twinkling glasses dwindle,
The waltzes and the croupiers' voices crumble,
The evening folds like a kaleidoscope.
Against the splinters of a reeling landscape
This image still pursues us into time:
Jungfrau, the legendary virgin spire,
Consumes the mind with mingled snow and fire.

RELIQUARY

The bones of saints are praised above their flesh,
That pale rejected garment of their lives
In which they walked despised, uncanonized.

Brooding upon the marble bones of time
Men read strange sanctity in lost events,
Hold requiem mass for murdered yesterdays,
And in the dust of actions once reviled
Find symbols traced, and freeze them into stone.

PURELY LOCAL

Beside this door a January tree
Answers a few days' warmth with shoots of green;
And knowing what the winds must do, I see
A hint of something human in the scene.
No matter how the almanacs have said
Hold back, distrust a purely local May,
When did we ever learn to be afraid?
Why are we scarred with winter's thrust today?

A VIEW OF THE TERRACE

Under the green umbrellas
Drinking golden tea,
There sit the porcelain people
Who care for you but little
And not at all for me.

The afternoon in crinkles
Lies stiffly on the lawn
And we, two furtive exiles,
Watch from an upper window
With shutters not quite drawn.

The gilt and scalloped laughter
Reaches us through a glaze,
And almost we imagine
That if we threw a pebble
The shining scene would craze.

But stones are thrown by children,
And we by now too wise
To try again to splinter
The bright enamel people
Impervious to surprise.

BY NO MEANS NATIVE

"Yonder," they told him, "things are not the same."
He found it understated when he came.
His tongue, in hopes to find itself at home,
Caught up the twist of every idiom.
He learned the accent and the turn of phrase,
Studied like Latin texts the local ways.
He tasted till his palate knew their shape
The country's proudest bean, its master grape.
He never talked of fields remembered green,
Or seasons in his land of origin.

And still he felt there lay a bridgeless space
Between himself and natives of the place.
Their laughter came when his had long abated;
He struggled in allusions never stated.
The truth at last cried out to be confessed:
He must remain eternally a guest,
Never to wear the birthmark of their ways.
He could be studying native all his days
And die a kind of minor alien still.
He might deceive himself by force of will,
Feel all the sentiments and give the sign,
Yet never overstep that tenuous line.

What else then? Wear the old identity,
The mark of other birth, and when you die,
Die as an exile? it has done for some.
Others surrender, book their passage home,
Only to seek their exile soon again,
No greater strangers than their countrymen.
Yet man will have his bondage to some place;
If not, he seeks an Order, or a race.

Some join the Masons, some embrace the Church,
And if they do, it does not matter much.

As for himself, he joined the band of those
Who pick their fruit no matter where it grows,
And learn to like it sweet or like it sour
Depending on the orchard or the hour.
By no means native, yet somewhat in love
With things a native is enamored of—
Except the sense of being held and owned
By one ancestral patch of local ground.

AIR WITHOUT INCENSE

We eat this body and remain ourselves.
We drink this liquor, tasting wine, not blood.
Among these triple icons, rites of seven,
We know the feast to be of earth, not heaven:
Here man is wounded, yet we speak of God.
More than the Nazarene with him was laid
Into the tomb, and in the tomb has stayed.

Communion of no saints, mass without bell,
Air without incense, we implore at need.
There are questions to be answered, and the sky
Answers no questions, hears no litany.
We breathe the vapors of a sickened creed.
Ours are assassins deadlier than sin;
Deeper disorders starve the soul within.

If any writ could tell us, we would read.
If any ghost dared lay on us a claim,
Our fibers would respond, our nerves obey;
But revelation moves apart today
From gestures of a tired pontifical game.
We seek, where lamp and kyrie expire,
A site unscourged by wasting tongues of fire.

FOR THE FELLING OF AN ELM
IN THE HARVARD YARD

They say the ground precisely swept
No longer feeds with rich decay
The roots enormous in their age
That long and deep beneath have slept.

So the great spire is overthrown,
And sharp saws have gone hurtling through
The rings that three slow centuries wore;
The second oldest elm is down.

The shade where James and Whitehead strolled
Becomes a litter on the green.
The young men pause along the paths
To see the axes glinting bold.

Watching the hewn trunk dragged away,
Some turn the symbol to their own,
And some admire the clean dispatch
With which the aged elm came down.

A CLOCK IN THE SQUARE

This handless clock stares blindly from its tower,
Refusing to acknowledge any hour.
But what can one clock do to stop the game
When others go on striking just the same?
Whatever mite of truth the gesture held,
Time may be silenced but will not be stilled,
Nor we absolved by any one's withdrawing
From all the restless ways we must be going
And all the rings in which we're spun and swirled,
Whether around a clockface or a world.

WHY ELSE BUT TO FORESTALL
THIS HOUR

Why else but to forestall this hour, I stayed
Out of the noonday sun, kept from the rain,
Swam only in familiar depths, and played
No hand where caution signaled to refrain?

For fourteen friends I walked behind the bier;
A score of cousins wilted in my sight.
I heard the steeples clang for each new year,
Then drew my shutters close against the night.

Bankruptcy fell on others like a dew;
Spendthrifts of life, they all succumbed and fled.
I did not chide them with the things I knew:
Smiling, I passed the almshouse of the dead.

I am the man who has outmisered death,
In pains and cunning laid my seasons by.
Now I must toil to win each hour and breath;
I am too full of years to reason why.

THIS BEAST, THIS ANGEL

No: this, my love, is neither you nor I.
This is the beast or angel, changing form,
The will that we are scourged and nourished by.

The golden fangs, the tall seraphic sword,
Alike unsheathed, await the midnight cry,
Blazon their answer to the stammered word.

Beneath this gaze our powers are fused as one;
We meet these eyes under the curve of night.
This is the transformation that is done

Where mortal forces slay mortality
And, towering at terrible full height,
This beast, this angel is both you and I.

EASTPORT TO BLOCK ISLAND

Along the coastal waters, signals run
In waves of caution and anxiety.
We'll try the catboat out another day.
So Danny stands in sea-grass by the porch
To watch a heeling dinghy, lone on grey,
Grapple with moods of wind that take the bay.

One year we walked among the shipwrecked shingles
Of storm-crazed cottages along the dune.
Rosa Morelli found her husband's boat
Ruined on the rocks; she never saw him dead,
And after seven years of stubborn hope
Began to curse the sight of things afloat.

The mother of the Kennedy boys is out
Stripping the Monday burden from the line
And looking for a rowboat round the headland.
Wonder if they stopped for bait at Mory's
And if the old man made them understand
This is a day for boys to stay on land?

Small craft, small craft, stay in and wait for tidings.
The word comes in with every hour of wind.
News of a local violence pricks the air,
And we who have seen the kitchen blown away,
Or Harper's children washed from sight, prepare
As usual in these parts for foul, not fair.

AT A DEATHBED IN THE
YEAR TWO THOUSAND

I bid you cast out pity.
No more of that: let be
Impotent grief and mourning.
How shall a man break free
From this deathwatch of earth,
This world estranged from mirth?

Show me gay faces only.
I call for pride and wit—
Men who remember laughter,
Brave jesters to befit
An age that would destroy
Its last outpost of joy.

No longer condolence
And wailing on the tongue.
An old man bids you laugh;
This text I leave the young:
Your rage and loud despair
But shake a crumbling stair.

Laughter is what men learn
At seventy years or more,
Weary of being stern
Or violent as before.
Laughter to us is left
To light that darkening rift

Where little time is with us,
Let us enact again
Not *Oedipus* but *The Clouds*.
Summon the players in.
Be proud on a sorry earth:
Bring on the men of mirth.

AFTERWARD

Now that your hopes are shamed, you stand
At last believing and resigned,
And none of us who touch your hand
Know how to give you back in kind
The words you flung when hopes were proud:
Being born to happiness
Above the asking of the crowd,
You would not take a finger less.
We who know limits now give room
To one who grows to fit her doom.

THE UNCLE SPEAKS IN THE DRAWING ROOM

I have seen the mob of late
Standing sullen in the square,
Gazing with a sullen stare
At window, balcony, and gate.
Some have talked in bitter tones,
Some have held and fingered stones.

These are follies that subside.
Let us consider, none the less,
Certain frailties of glass
Which, it cannot be denied,
Lead in times like these to fear
For crystal vase and chandelier.

Not that missiles will be cast;
None as yet dare lift an arm.
But the scene recalls a storm
When our grandsire stood aghast
To see his antique ruby bowl
Shivered in a thunder-roll.

Let us only bear in mind
How these treasures handed down
From a calmer age passed on
Are in the keeping of our kind.
We stand between the dead glass-blowers
And murmurings of missile-throwers.

BOUNDARY

What has happened here will do
To bite the living world in two,
Half for me and half for you.
Here at last I fix a line
Severing the world's design
Too small to hold both yours and mine.
There's enormity in a hair
Enough to lead men not to share
Narrow confines of a sphere
But put an ocean or a fence
Between two opposite intents.
A hair would span the difference.

FIVE O'CLOCK, BEACON HILL

Curtis and I sit drinking auburn sherry
In the receptive twilight of the vines
And potted exile shrubs with sensitive spines
Greening the glass of the conservatory.

Curtis, in sand-grey coat and tie of madder,
Meets elder values with polite negation.
I, between yew and lily, in resignation
Watch lime-green shade across his left cheek spatter.

Gazing beyond my elbow, he allows
Significance of sorts to Baudelaire.
His phrases float across the lucent air
Like exotic leaves detached from waxy boughs.

I drink old sherry and look at Curtis' nose—
Intelligent Puritan feature, grave, discreet,
Unquestionably a nose that one might meet
In portraits of antique generalissimos.

The study seems sufficient recompense
For Curtis' dissertations upon Gide.
What rebel breathes beneath his mask, indeed?
Avant-garde in tradition's lineaments!

FROM A CHAPTER
ON LITERATURE

After the sunlight and the fiery vision
Leading us to a place of running water,
We came into a place by water altered.
Dew ribboned from those trees, the grasses wept
And drowned in their own weeping; vacant mist
Crawled like a snail across the land, and left
A snail's moist trace; and everything there thriving
Stared through an aqueous half-light, without mirth
And bred by languid cycles, without ardor.

There passion mildewed and corrupted slowly,
Till, feeding hourly on its own corruption,
It had forgotten fire and aspiration,
Becoming sodden with appetite alone.
There in the green-grey thickness of the air
Lived and begat cold spores of intellect,
Till giant mosses of a rimelike aspect
Hung heavily from the boughs to testify
Against all simple sensualities,
Turning them by a touch gross and discolored,
Swelling the warm taut flesh to bloated symbol
By unrelenting watery permeations.

So from promethean hopes we came this far,
This far from lands of sun and racing blood.
Behind us lay the blazing apple tree,
Behind us too the vulture and the rock—
The tragic labor and the heroic doom—
For without passion the rock also crumbles
And the wet twilight scares the bird away.

AN UNSAID WORD

She who has power to call her man
From that estranged intensity
Where his mind forages alone,
Yet keeps her peace and leaves him free,
And when his thoughts to her return
Stands where he left her, still his own,
Knows this the hardest thing to learn.

MATHILDE IN NORMANDY

From the archaic ships the green and red
Invaders woven in their colored hosts
Descend to conquer. Here is the threaded headland,
The warp and woof of a tideless beach, the flight,
Recounted by slow shuttles, of swift arrows,
And the outlandish attitudes of death
In the stitched soldiery. That this should prove
More than the personal episode, more than all
The little lives sketched on the teeming loom
Was then withheld from you; self-conscious history
That writes deliberate footnotes to its action
Was not of your young epoch. For a pastime
The patient handiwork of long-sleeved ladies
Was esteemed proper when their lords abandoned
The fields and apple trees of Normandy
For harsher hunting on the opposite coast.
Yours was a time when women sat at home
To the pleasing minor airs of lute and hautbois,
While the bright sun on the expensive threads
Glowed in the long windless afternoons.

Say what you will, anxiety there too
Played havoc with the skein, and the knots came
When fingers' occupation and mind's attention
Grew too divergent, at the keen remembrance
Of wooden ships putting out from a long beach,
And the grey ocean dimming to a void,
And the sick strained farewells, too sharp for speech.

AT A BACH CONCERT

Coming by evening through the wintry city
We said that art is out of love with life.
Here we approach a love that is not pity.

This antique discipline, tenderly severe,
Renews belief in love yet masters feeling,
Asking of us a grace in what we bear.

Form is the ultimate gift that love can offer—
The vital union of necessity
With all that we desire, all that we suffer.

A too-compassionate art is half an art.
Only such proud restraining purity
Restores the else-betrayed, too-human heart.

THE RAIN OF BLOOD

In that dark year an angry rain came down
Blood-red upon the hot stones of the town.
Beneath the pelting of that liquid drought
No garden stood, no shattered stalk could sprout,
As from a sunless sky all day it rained
And men came in from streets of terror stained
With that unnatural ichor. Under night
Impatient lovers did not quench the light,
But listening heard above each other's breath
That sound the dying heard in rooms of death.
Each loudly asked abroad, and none dared tell
What omen in that burning torrent fell.
And all night long we lay, while overhead
The drops rained down as if the heavens bled;
And every dawn we woke to hear the sound,
And all men knew that they could stanch the wound,
But each looked out and cursed the stricken town,
The guilty roofs on which the rain came down.

STEPPING BACKWARD

Good-by to you whom I shall see tomorrow,
Next year and when I'm fifty; still good-by.
This is the leave we never really take.
If you were dead or gone to live in China
The event might draw your stature in my mind.
I should be forced to look upon you whole
The way we look upon the things we lose.
We see each other daily and in segments;
Parting might make us meet anew, entire.

You asked me once, and I could give no answer,
How far dare we throw off the daily ruse,
Official treacheries of face and name,
Have out our true identity? I could hazard
An answer now, if you are asking still.
We are a small and lonely human race
Showing no sign of mastering solitude
Out on this stony planet that we farm.
The most that we can do for one another
Is let our blunders and our blind mischances
Argue a certain brusque abrupt compassion.
We might as well be truthful. I should say
They're luckiest who know they're not unique;
But only art or common interchange
Can teach that kindest truth. And even art
Can only hint at what disturbed a Melville
Or calmed a Mahler's frenzy; you and I
Still look from separate windows every morning
Upon the same white daylight in the square.

And when we come into each other's rooms
Once in awhile, encumbered and self-conscious,
We hover awkwardly about the threshold
And usually regret the visit later.
Perhaps the harshest fact is, only lovers—
And once in awhile two with the grace of lovers—
Unlearn that clumsiness of rare intrusion
And let each other freely come and go.
Most of us shut too quickly into cupboards
The margin-scribbled books, the dried geranium,
The penny horoscope, letters never mailed.
The door may open, but the room is altered;
Not the same room we look from night and day.

It takes a late and slowly blooming wisdom
To learn that those we marked infallible
Are tragi-comic stumblers like ourselves.
The knowledge breeds reserve. We walk on tiptoe,
Demanding more than we know how to render.
Two-edged discovery hunts us finally down;
The human act will make us real again,
And then perhaps we come to know each other.

Let us return to imperfection's school.
No longer wandering after Plato's ghost,
Seeking the garden where all fruit is flawless,
We must at last renounce that ultimate blue
And take a walk in other kinds of weather.
The sourest apple makes its wry announcement
That imperfection has a certain tang.
Maybe we shouldn't turn our pockets out
To the last crumb or lingering bit of fluff,
But all we can confess of what we are
Has in it the defeat of isolation—
If not our own, then someone's, anyway.

So I come back to saying this good-by,
A sort of ceremony of my own,
This stepping backward for another glance.
Perhaps you'll say we need no ceremony,
Because we know each other, crack and flaw,
Like two irregular stones that fit together.
Yet still good-by, because we live by inches
And only sometimes see the full dimension.
Your stature's one I want to memorize—
Your whole level of being, to impose
On any other comers, man or woman.
I'd ask them that they carry what they are
With your particular bearing, as you wear
The flaws that make you both yourself and human.

ITINERARY

The guidebooks play deception; oceans are
A property of mind. All maps are fiction,
All travelers come to separate frontiers.

The coast, they said, is barren; birds go over
Unlighting, in search of richer inland gardens.
No green weed thrusts its tendril from the rock face.

Visit it if you must; then turn again
To the warm pleasing air of colored towns
Where rivers wind to lace the summer valleys.

The coast is naked, sharp with cliffs, unkind,
They said; scrub-bitten. Inland there are groves
And fêtes of light and music.

                            But I have seen

Such denizens of enchantment print these sands
As seldom prowl the margins of old charts:
Stallions of verd antique and wild brown children
And tails of mermaids glittering through the sea!

A REVIVALIST IN BOSTON

But you shall walk the golden street,
And you unhouse and house the Lord.

—Gerard Manley Hopkins

Going home by lamplight across Boston Common,
We heard him tell how God had entered in him,
And now he had the Word, and nothing other
Would do but he must cry it to his brother.

We stood and listened there—to nothing new.
Yet something loosed his tongue and drove him shouting.
Compulsion's not play-acted in a face,
And he was telling us the way to grace.

Somehow we saw the youth that he had been,
Not one to notice; an ordinary boy—
Hardly the one the Lord would make His tool—
Shuffling his feet in Baptist Sunday school.

And then transfiguration came his way;
He knew the secret all the rest were seeking.
He made the tale of Christendom his own,
And hoarsely called his brethren to the throne.

The same old way; and yet we knew he saw
The angelic hosts whose names he stumbled over.
He made us hear the ranks of shining feet
Treading to glory's throne up Tremont Street.

THE RETURN OF THE
EVENING GROSBEAKS

The birds about the house pretend to be
Penates of our domesticity.
And when the cardinal wants to play at prophet
We never tell his eminence to come off it.

The crows, too, in the dawn prognosticate
Like ministers at a funeral of state.
The pigeons in their surplices of white
Assemble for some careful Anglican rite.

Only these guests who rarely come our way
Dictate no oracles for us while they stay.
No matter what we try to make them mean
Their coming lends no answer to our scene.

We scatter seed and call them by their name,
Remembering what has changed since last they came.

THE SPRINGBOARD

Like divers, we ourselves must make the jump
That sets the taut board bounding underfoot
Clean as an axe blade driven in a stump;
But afterward what makes the body shoot
Into its pure and irresistible curve
Is of a force beyond all bodily powers.
So action takes velocity with a verve
Swifter, more sure than any will of ours.

A CHANGE OF WORLD

Fashions are changing in the sphere.
Oceans are asking wave by wave
What new shapes will be worn next year;
And the mountains, stooped and grave,
Are wondering silently range by range
What if they prove too old for the change.

The little tailors busily sitting
Flashing their shears in rival haste
Won't spare time for a prior fitting—
In with the stitches, too late to baste.
They say the season for doubt has passed:
The changes coming are due to last.

UNSOUNDED

Mariner unpracticed,
In this chartless zone
Every navigator
Fares unwarned, alone.
Each his own Magellan
In tropics of sensation:
Not a fire-scorched stone
From prior habitation,
Not an archaic hull
Splintered on the beach.
These are latitudes revealed
Separate to each.

DESIGN IN LIVING COLORS

Embroidered in a tapestry of green
Among the textures of a threaded garden,
The gesturing lady and her paladin
Walk in a path where shade and sunlight harden
Upon the formal attitudes of trees
By no wind bent, and birds without a tune,
Against the background of a figured frieze
In an eternal summer afternoon.

So you and I in our accepted frame
Believe a casual world of bricks and flowers
And scarcely guess what symbols wander tame
Among the panels of familiar hours.
Yet should the parting boughs of green reveal
A slender unicorn with jeweled feet,
Could I persuade him at my touch to kneel
And from my fingers take what unicorns eat?

If you should pick me at my whim a rose,
Setting the birds upon the bush in flight,
How should I know what crimson meaning grows
Deep in this garden, where such birds alight?
And how should I believe, the meaning clear,
That we are children of disordered days?
That fragmentary world is mended here,
And in this air a clearer sunlight plays.

The fleeing hare, the wings that brush the tree,
All images once separate and alone,
Become the creatures of a tapestry
Miraculously stirred and made our own.
We are the denizens of a living wood
Where insight blooms anew on every bough,
And every flower emerges understood
Out of a pattern unperceived till now.

WALDEN 1950

Thoreau, lank ghost, comes back to visit Concord,
Finds the town like all towns, much the same—
A little less remote, less independent.
The cars hurl through from dawn to dawn toward Boston
Paying out speed like a lifeline between towns.
Some of them pause to look at Alcott's house.
No farmer studies Latin now; the language
Of soil and market would confound a scholar;
And any Yankee son with lonesome notions
Would find life harder in the town today.

Under the trees by Walden Pond, the stalls
Where summer pilgrims pause beside the road,
Drown resinous night in busy rivalry
While the young make boisterous love along the shores.

He used to hear the locomotive whistle
Sound through the woods like a hawk's restless cry.
Now the trains run through Concord night and day,
And nobody stops to listen. The ghost might smile—
The way a man in solitude would smile—
Remembering all the sounds that passed for sound
A century ago.
                    He would remain
Away from houses other ghosts might visit,
Not having come to tell a thing or two
Or lay a curse (what curse could frighten now?)
No tapping on the windowpane for him
Or twilight conversation in the streets
With some bewildered townsman going home.

If he had any errand, it would be
More likely curiosity of his own
About the human race, at least in Concord.
He would not come so far from distant woods
Merely to set them wondering again.

SUNDAY EVENING

We are two acquaintances on a train,
Rattling back through darkening twilight suburbs
From a weekend in the country, into town.
The station lights flare past us, and we glance
Furtively at our watches, sit upright
On leather benches in the smoke-dim car
And try to make appropriate conversation.

We come from similar streets in the same city
And have spent this same hiatus of three days
Escaping streets and lives that we have chosen.
Escape by deck chairs sprawled on evening lawns,
By citronella and by visitant moths;
Escape by sand and water in the eyes,
And sea-noise drowned in weekend conversation.

Uneasy, almost, that we meet again,
Impatient for this rattling ride to end,
We still are stricken with a dread of passing
Time, the coming loneliness of travelers
Parting in hollow stations, going home
To silent rooms in too-familiar streets
With unknown footsteps pacing overhead.

For there are things we might have talked about,
And there are signs we might have shared in common.
We look out vainly at the passing stations
As if some lamplit shed or gleaming roof
Might reawake the sign in both of us.
But this is only Rye or Darien,
And whoever we both knew there has moved away.

And I suppose there never will be time
To speak of more than this—the change in weather,
The lateness of the train on Sunday evenings—
Never enough or always too much time.
Life lurches past us like a windowed twilight
Seen from a train that halts at little junctions
Where weekend half-acquaintances say good-by.

THE INNOCENTS

They said to us, or tried to say, and failed:

With dust implicit in the uncurled green
First leaf, and all the early garden knowing
That after rose-red petals comes the bleak
Impoverished stalk, the black dejected leaf
Crumpled and dank, we should at Maytime be
Less childlike in delight, a little reserved,
A little cognizant of rooted death.

And yet beneath the flecked leaf-gilded boughs
Along the paths fern-fringed and delicate,
We supple children played at golden age,
And knelt upon the curving steps to snare
The whisking emerald lizards, or to coax
The ancestral tortoise from his onyx shell
In lemon sunlight on the balcony.
And only pedagogues and the brittle old
Existed to declare mortality,
And they were beings removed in walk and speech.

For apprehension feeds on intellect:
Uneasy ghosts in libraries are bred—
While innocent sensuality abides
In charmed perception of an hour, a day,
Ingenuous and unafraid of time.

So in the garden we were free of fear,
And what the saffron roses or the green
Imperial dragonflies above the lake
Knew about altered seasons, boughs despoiled,
They never murmured; and to us no matter
How in the drawing room the elders sat

Balancing teacups behind curtained glass,
While rare miraculous clocks in crystal domes
Impaled the air with splintered chips of time
Forever sounding through the tea-thin talk,
An organpoint to desperate animation.

They knew, and tried to say to us, but failed;
They knew what we would never have believed.

"HE REMEMBERETH THAT WE ARE DUST"

And when was dust a thing so rash?
Or when could dust support the lash
And stand as arrogant as stone?
And where has revelation shown
Conceit and rage so interfused
In dust, that suns have stood bemused
To watch the reckless consequence?
And when did dust break reticence
To sing aloud with all its might
In egotistical delight?
Yet when the tale is told of wind
That lifted dust and drove behind
To scoop the valleys from their sleep
And bury landscapes inches deep
Till there must follow years of rain
Before the earth could breathe again—
Or when the appetite of fire
Blazes beyond control and higher,
Then sinks into the sullen waste
Of what, devouring, it effaced,
And thinly in my palm I hold
The dust of ash grown wan and cold,
I know what element I chose
To build such anger, mould such woes.

LIFE AND LETTERS

An old man's wasting brain; a ruined city
Where here and there against the febrile sky
The shaft of an unbroken column rises,
And in the sands indifferent lizards keep
The shattered traces of old monuments.
Here where the death of the imagination
Trances the mind with shadow, here the shapes
Of tumbled arch and pediment stand out
In their last violence of illumination.

By day his valet rules him, forcing him
With milk and medicines, a deference
Cloaking the bully. "Signora X was here
During your nap; I told her doctor's orders,
You must stay quiet and rest, keep up your strength."
He leaves the pasteboard rectangle, engraved,
Scrawled in regretful haste, and goes his way
To join a lounging crony belowstairs.
("The old man's not so wide awake today.")

The ivory body in the dressing gown
(Not the silk robe the Countess sent; he spills
His milk sometimes, and that would be a pity)
Stirs in the sinking warmth that bathes his chair
And looks on summer sunlight in the square.
Below, the fat concierge points out his window
With half-drawn blinds, to tourists who inquire.
There are a few who make the pilgrimage;
They stand and gaze and go away again.
Something to say that one has stood beneath
His window, though they never see himself.
The post brings letters stamped in foreign countries.
He holds them in his fingers, turns them over.

"He always says he means to read them later,
But I should say his reading days are finished.
All he does now is watch the square below.
He seems content enough; and I've no trouble.
An easy life, to watch him to his grave."

The letters still arrive from universities,
Occasionally a charitable cause,
A favor-seeker, or an aged friend.
But now it seems no answers are expected
From one whose correspondence is collected
In two large volumes, edited with notes.
What should that timid hand beneath its sleeve
Warmed by the rich Italian sun, indite
To vindicate its final quarter-decade?
No; he has written all that can be known.
If anything, too much; his greedy art
Left no domain unpillaged, grew its breadth
From fastening on every life he touched.
(Some went to law, some smiled, some never guessed.)
But now the art has left the man to rest.

The failing searchlight of his mind remains
To throw its wavering cone of recognition
Backward upon those teeming images.
New York invades the memory again:
A million jewels crowd the boyish brain
With apprehensions of an unmastered world.
The red-haired girl waves from the Brooklyn ferry,
The bridges leap like fountains into noon.
Again the train goes rocking across-country
Past midnight platforms where the reddish light
Plays on a game of checkers through the window,
Till dawn spells snow on emptiness of plains.

Once more in San Francisco Margaret wakes
Beside him in the heat of August dark,
Still weeping from a nightmare.
                                        So by day
He looks on summer sunlight in the square.

The grinning Bacchus trickles from his gourd
A thin bright spume of water in the basin,
While the hot tiles grow cool as evening drops
Deep cobalt from white buildings. Far in air
Buonarroti's dome delays the gold.
The old man who has come to Rome to die
Ignores the death of still another day.
So many days have died and come to life
That time and place seem ordered by his valet;
He puts them on and off as he is told.

Now he is standing bareheaded in dusk
While fireworks rain into the sea at Biarritz,
And at his shoulder Louis Scarapin
Quotes La Fontaine. The giddy winds of fortune
Make love to him that night; and he recalls
Toasts drunk by rocketlight, and Louis' voice
With its perpetual drawl: *"Mon bon monsieur . . ."*
Louis, who could have made the world more sane,
But killed himself instead, a Pierrot-gesture,
His face a whiteness in the dark apartment.

The bitter coffee drunk on early mornings
With Sandra's straw hat hanging from the bedpost,
Red roses, like a bonnet by Renoir.
And the incessant tapping of her heels
Late evenings on the cobbles as they stroll:
Splinters to tingle in an old man's brain.

Again the consumptive neighbor through the wall
Begins his evening agony of coughing
Till one is ready to scream him into silence.
And the accordion on the river steamer
Plays something from last season, foolish, gay;
Deaf ears preserve the music of a day.

Life has the final word; he cannot rule
Those floating pictures as he ruled them once,
Forcing them into form; the violent gardener,
The two-edged heart that cuts into every wound,
Reciprocates experience with art.
No more of that for now; the boughs grow wild,
The willful stems put forth undisciplined blooms,
And winds sweep through and shatter. Here at last
Anarchy of a thousand roses tangles
The fallen architecture of the mind.

FOR THE CONJUNCTION OF TWO PLANETS

We smile at astrological hopes
And leave the sky to expert men
Who do not reckon horoscopes
But painfully extend their ken
In mathematical debate
With slide and photographic plate.

And yet, protest it if we will,
Some corner of the mind retains
The medieval man, who still
Keeps watch upon those starry skeins
And drives us out of doors at night
To gaze at anagrams of light.

Whatever register or law
Is drawn in digits for these two,
Venus and Jupiter keep their awe,
Wardens of brilliance, as they do
Their dual circuit of the west—
The brightest planet and her guest.

Is any light so proudly thrust
From darkness on our lifted faces
A sign of something we can trust,
Or is it that in starry places
We see the things we long to see
In fiery iconography?

POEMS

(1 9 5 0 – 1 9 5 1)

THE PRISONERS

Enclosed in this disturbing mutual wood,
Wounded alike by thorns of the same tree,
We seek in hopeless war each others' blood
Though suffering in one identity.
Each to the other prey and huntsman known,
Still driven together, lonelier than alone.

Strange mating of the loser and the lost!
With faces stiff as mourners', we intrude
Forever on the one each turns from most,
Each wandering in a double solitude.
The unpurged ghosts of passion bound by pride
Who wake in isolation, side by side.

1950

NIGHT

The motes that still disturbed her lidded calm
Were these: the tick and whisper of a shade
Against the sill; a cobweb-film that hung
Aslant a corner moulding, too elusive
For any but the gaze of straitened eyes;
The nimbus of the night-lamp, where a moth
Uneasily explored the edge of light
Through hours of fractured darkness. She alone
Knew that the room contained these things; she lay
Hearing the almost imperceptible sound
(As if a live thing shivered behind the curtains)
Watching the thread that frayed in gusts of air
More delicate than her breathing, or by night
Sharing a moth's perplexity at light
Too frail to drive out dark: minutiae
Held in the vise of sense about to die.

1950

THE HOUSE AT THE CASCADES

All changed now through neglect. The steps dismantled
By infantries of ants, by roots and storms,
The pillars tugged by vines, the porte-cochère
A passageway for winds, the solemn porches
Warped into caricatures.
                    We came at evening
After the rain, when every drunken leaf
Was straining, swelling in a riot of green.
Only the house was dying in all that life,
As if a triumph of emerald energy
Had fixed its mouth upon the walls and stones.
The tamest shrub remembered anarchy
And joined in appetite with the demagogue weed
That springs where order falls; together there
They stormed the defenseless handiwork of man
Whose empire wars against him when he turns
A moment from the yoke. So, turning back,
He sees his rooftree fall to furious green,
His yard despoiled, and out of innocent noon
The insect-cloud like thunder on the land.

1951

THE DIAMOND
CUTTERS

(1955)

For A. H. C.

THE ROADWAY

When the footbridge washes away,
And the lights along the bank
Accost each other no longer,
But the wild grass grows up rank,
And no one comes to stand
Where neighbor and neighbor stood,
And each house is drawn in to itself
And shuttered against the road,

Under each separate roof
The familiar life goes on:
The hearth is swept up at night,
The table laid in the dawn,
And man and woman and child
Eat their accustomed meal,
Give thanks and turn to their day
As if by an act of will.

Nowhere is evil spoken,
Though something deep in the heart
Refuses to mend the bridge
And can never make a start
Along the abandoned path
To the house at left or at right,
Where neighbor and neighbor's children
Awake to the same daylight.

Good men grown long accustomed
To inflexible ways of mind—
Which of them could say clearly
What first drove kind from kind?
Courteous to any stranger,
Forbearing with wife and child—
Yet along the common roadway
The wild grass still grows wild.

PICTURES BY VUILLARD

Now we remember all: the wild pear-tree,
The broken ribbons of the green-and-gold
Portfolio, with sketches from an old
Algerian campaign; the placid three
Women at coffee by the window, fates
Of nothing ominous, waiting for the ring
Of the postman's bell; we harbor everything—
The cores of fruit left on the luncheon plates.
We are led back where we have never been,
Midday where nothing's tragic, all's delayed
As it should have been for us as well—that shade
Of summer always, Neuilly dappled green!

But we, the destined readers of Stendhal,
In monstrous change such consolations find
As restless mockery sets before the mind
To deal with what must anger and appall.
Much of the time we scarcely think of sighing
For afternoons that found us born too late.
Our prudent envy rarely paces spying
Under those walls, that lilac-shadowed gate.
Yet at this moment, in our private view,
A breath of common peace, like memory,
Rustles the branches of the wild pear-tree—
Air that we should have known, and cannot know.

ORIENT WHEAT

Our fathers in their books and speech
Have made the matter plain:
The green fields they walked in once
Will never grow again.
The corn lies under the locust's tooth
Or blistered in the sun;
The faces of the old proud stock
Are gone where their years are gone.

The park where stags lay down at noon
Under the great trees
Is shrill with Sunday strollers now,
Littered with their lees.
Poachers have trampled down the maze
And choked the fountains dry;
The last swan of a score and ten
Goes among reeds to die.

We were born to smells of plague,
Chalk-marks on every door;
We never have heard the hunting-horn
Or feet on the gallery floor—
The high-arched feet of dancers
Who knew how to step and stand.
We were born of a leaning house
In a changed, uneasy land.

Our fathers curse the crooked time
And go to their graves at last;
While some of us laugh at doting men,
And others sigh for the past.
And the dazzled lovers lie
Where summer burns blue and green,
In the green fields they'll be saying
Can never grow again.

VERSAILLES
(Petit Trianon)

Merely the landscape of a vanished whim,
An artifice that lasts beyond the wish:
The grotto by the pond, the gulping fish
That round and round pretended islands swim,
The creamery abandoned to its doves,
The empty shrine the guidebooks say is love's.

What wind can bleaken this, what weather chasten
Those balustrades of stone, that sky stone-pale?
A fountain triton idly soaks his tail
In the last puddle of a drying basin;
A leisure that no human will can hasten
Drips from the hollow of his lifted shell.

When we were younger gardens were for games,
But now across the sungilt lawn of kings
We drift, consulting catalogues for names
Of postured gods: the cry of closing rings
For us and for the couples in the wood
And all good children who are all too good.

O children, next year, children, you will play
With only half your hearts; be wild today.
And lovers, take one long and fast embrace
Before the sun that tarnished queens goes down,
And evening finds you in a restless town
Where each has back his old restricted face.

ANNOTATION FOR AN EPITAPH

A fairer person lost not heaven.

—Paradise Lost

These are the sins for which they cast out angels,
The bagatelles by which the lovely fall:
A hand that disappoints, an eye dissembling—
These and a few besides: you had them all.

Beneath this cherubed stone reclines the beauty
That cherubs at the Chair will never see,
Shut out forever by the gold battalions
Stern to forgive, more rigorous than we.

Oh, we were quick to hide our eyes from foible
And call such beauty truth; what though we knew?
Never was truth so sweet and so outrageous;
We loved you all the more because untrue.

But in the baroque corridors of heaven
Your lively coming is a hope destroyed.
Squadrons of seraphs pass the news and ponder,
And all their luxury glitters grand and void.

IDEAL LANDSCAPE

We had to take the world as it was given:
The nursemaid sitting passive in the park
Was rarely by a changeling prince accosted.
The mornings happened similar and stark
In rooms of selfhood where we woke and lay
Watching today unfold like yesterday.

Our friends were not unearthly beautiful,
Nor spoke with tongues of gold; our lovers blundered
Now and again when most we sought perfection,
Or hid in cupboards when the heavens thundered.
The human rose to haunt us everywhere,
Raw, flawed, and asking more than we could bear.

And always time was rushing like a tram
Through streets of a foreign city, streets we saw
Opening into great and sunny squares
We could not find again, no map could show—
Never those fountains tossed in that same light,
Those gilded trees, those statues green and white.

THE CELEBRATION
IN THE PLAZA

The sentimentalist sends his mauve balloon
Meandering into air. The crowd applauds.
The mayor eats ices with a cardboard spoon.

See how that color charms the sunset air;
A touch of lavender is what was needed.—
Then, pop! no floating lavender anywhere.

Hurrah, the pyrotechnic engineer
Comes with his sparkling tricks, consults the sky,
Waits for the perfect instant to appear.

Bouquets of gold splash into bloom and pour
Their hissing pollen downward on the dusk.
Nothing like this was ever seen before.

The viceroy of fireworks goes his way,
Leaving us with a sky so dull and bare
The crowd thins out: what conjures them to stay?

The road is cold with dew, and by and by
We see the constellations overhead.
But is that all? some little children cry.

All we have left, their pedagogues reply.

THE TOURIST AND THE TOWN
(San Miniato al Monte)

Those clarities detached us, gave us form,
Made us like architecture. Now no more
Bemused by local mist, our edges blurred,
We knew where we began and ended. There
We were the campanile and the dome,
Alive and separate in that bell-struck air,
Climate whose light reformed our random line,
Edged our intent and sharpened our desire.

Could it be always so—a week of sunlight,
Walks with a guidebook, picking out our way
Through verbs and ruins, yet finding after all
The promised vista, once!—The light has changed
Before we can make it ours. We have no choice:
We are only tourists under that blue sky,
Reading the posters on the station wall—
Come, take a walking-trip through happiness.

There is a mystery that floats between
The tourist and the town. Imagination
Estranges it from her. She need not suffer
Or die here. It is none of her affair,
Its calm heroic vistas make no claim.
Her bargains with disaster have been sealed
In another country. Here she goes untouched,
And this is alienation. Only sometimes
In certain towns she opens certain letters
Forwarded on from bitter origins,
That send her walking, sick and haunted, through
Mysterious and ordinary streets
That are no more than streets to walk and walk—
And then the tourist and the town are one.

To work and suffer is to be at home.
All else is scenery: the Rathaus fountain,
The skaters in the sunset on the lake
At Salzburg, or, emerging after snow,
The singular clear stars at Castellane.
To work and suffer is to come to know
The angles of a room, light in a square,
As convalescents know the face of one
Who has watched beside them. Yours now, every street,
The noonday swarm across the bridge, the bells
Bruising the air above the crowded roofs,
The avenue of chestnut-trees, the road
To the post-office. Once upon a time
All these for you were fiction. Now, made free
You live among them. Your breath is on this air,
And you are theirs and of their mystery.

BEARS

Wonderful bears that walked my room all night,
Where are you gone, your sleek and fairy fur,
Your eyes' veiled imperious light?

Brown bears as rich as mocha or as musk,
White opalescent bears whose fur stood out
Electric in the deepening dusk,

And great black bears who seemed more blue than black,
More violet than blue against the dark—
Where are you now? upon what track

Mutter your muffled paws, that used to tread
So softly, surely, up the creakless stair
While I lay listening in bed?

When did I lose you? whose have you become?
Why do I wait and wait and never hear
Your thick nocturnal pacing in my room?
My bears, who keeps you now, in pride and fear?

THE INSUSCEPTIBLES

Then the long sunlight lying on the sea
Fell, folded gold on gold; and slowly we
Took up our decks of cards, our parasols,
The picnic hamper and the sandblown shawls
And climbed the dunes in silence. There were two
Who lagged behind as lovers sometimes do,
And took a different road. For us the night
Was final, and by artificial light
We came indoors to sleep. No envy there
Of those who might be watching anywhere
The lustres of the summer dark, to trace
Some vagrant splinter blazing out of space.
No thought of them, save in a lower room
To leave a light for them when they should come.

LUCIFER IN THE TRAIN

Riding the black express from heaven to hell
He bit his fingers, watched the countryside,
Vernal and crystalline, forever slide
Beyond his gaze: the long cascades that fell
Ribboned in sunshine from their sparkling height,
The fishers fastened to their pools of green
By silver lines; the birds in sudden flight—
All things the diabolic eye had seen
Since heaven's cockcrow. Imperceptibly
That landscape altered: now in paler air
Tree, hill and rock stood out resigned, severe,
Beside the strangled field, the stream run dry.

Lucifer, we are yours who stiff and mute
Ride out of worlds we shall not see again,
And watch from windows of a smoking train
The ashen prairies of the absolute.
Once out of heaven, to an angel's eye
Where is the bush or cloud without a flaw?
What bird but feeds upon mortality,
Flies to its young with carrion in its claw?
O foundered angel, first and loneliest
To turn this bitter sand beneath your hoe,
Teach us, the newly-landed, what you know;
After our weary transit, find us rest.

RECORDERS IN ITALY

It was amusing on that antique grass,
Seated halfway between the green and blue,
To waken music gentle and extinct

Under the old walls where the daisies grew
Sprinkled in cinquecento style, as though
Archangels might have stepped there yesterday.

But it was we, mortal and young, who strolled
And fluted quavering music, for a day
Casual heirs of all we looked upon.

Such pipers of the emerald afternoon
Could only be the heirs of perfect time
When every leaf distinctly brushed with gold

Listened to Primavera speaking flowers.
Those scherzos stumble now; our journeys run
To harsher hillsides, rockier declensions.

Obligatory climates call us home.
And so shall clarity of cypresses,
Unfingered by necessity, become

Merely the ghost of half-remembered trees,
A trick of sunlight flattering the mind?—
There were four recorders sweet upon the wind.

AT HERTFORD HOUSE

Perfection now is tended and observed,
Not used; we hire the spawn of Caliban
For daily service. In our careful world
Inlay of purple-wood and tulip, curved
To mime the sheen of plumes and peacocks' eyes,
Exists for inspection only. And the jars
Of apple-green and white, where wooing's done
In panels after Boucher—such we prize
Too well to fill with roses. Chocolate, too,
Will not again be frothed in cups like these;
We move meticulously, ill at ease
Amid perfections. Why should a porcelain plaque
Where Venus pulls her pouting Adon on
Through beds of blushing flowers, seem unfit
For casual thumbprint? Ease is what we lack.
There's a division nothing can make sweet
Between the clods of usage and the toys
We strum our senses with. But Antoinette
Ran her long tortoise-shell and silver comb
Through powdered yellow hair, and would have laughed
To think that use too mean for art or craft.

THE WILD SKY

Here from the corridor of an English train,
I see the landscape slide through glancing rain,
A land so personal that every leaf
Unfolds as if to witness human life,
And every aging milestone seems to know
That human hands inscribed it, long ago.

Oasthouse and garden, narrow bridge and hill—
Landscape with figures, where a change of style
Comes softened in a water-colour light
By Constable; and always, shire on shire,
The low-pitched sky sags like a tent of air
Beneath its ancient immaterial weight.

The weather in these gentle provinces
Moves like the shift of daylight in a house,
Subdued by time and custom. Sun and rain
Are intimate, complaisant to routine,
Guests in the garden. Year on country year
Has worn the edge of wildness from this air.

And I remember that unblunted light
Poured out all day from a prodigious height—
My country, where the blue is miles too high
For minds of men to graze the leaning sky.
The telegraph may rise or timber fall,
That last frontier remains, the vertical.

Men there are beanstalk climbers, all day long
Haunted by stilts they clattered on when young.
Giants no longer, now at mortal size
They stare into that upward wilderness.
The vertical reminds them what they are,
And I remember I am native there.

THE PROSPECT

You promise me when certain things are done
We'll close these rooms above a city square,
And stealing out by half-light, will be gone
When next the telephone breaks the waiting air.
Before they send to find us, we shall be
Aboard a blunt-nosed steamer, at whose rail
We'll watch the loading of the last brown bale
And feel the channel roughening into sea

And after many sunlit days we'll sight
The coast you tell me of. Along that shore
Rare shells lie tumbled, and the seas of light
Dip past the golden rocks to crash and pour
Upon the bowl-shaped beach. In that clear bay
We'll scoop for pebbles till our feet and hands
Are gilded by the wash of blending sands;
And though the boat lift anchor, we shall stay.

You will discover in the woods beyond
The creatures you have loved on Chinese silk:
The shell-gray fox, gazelles that at your sound
Will lift their eyes as calm as golden milk.
The leaves and grasses feathered into plumes
Will shadow-edge their pale calligraphy;
And in the evening you will come to me
To tell of honey thick in silver combs.

Yet in the drift of moments unendeared
By sameness, when the cracks of morning show
Only a replica of days we've marred
With still the same old penances to do,
In furnished rooms above a city square,
Eating the rind of fact, I sometimes dread
The promise of that honey-breeding air,
Those unapportioned clusters overhead.

EPILOGUE FOR A
MASQUE OF PURCELL

Beast and bird must bow aside,
Grimbald limp into the wings.
All that's lovely and absurd,
All that dances, all that sings

Folded into trunks again—
The haunted grove, the starlit air
All turns workaday and plain,
Even the happy, happy pair.

Harpsichord and trumpet go
Trundling down the dusty hall.
That airy joy, that postured woe
Like the black magician's spell

Fall in pieces round us now,
While the dancer goes to lie
With the king, and need not know
He will jilt her by and by.

We were young once and are old;
Have seen the dragon die before;
Knew the innocent and bold,
Saw them through the cardboard door

Kiss the guilty and afraid,
Turning human soon enough.
We have wept with the betrayed,
Never known them die for love.

Yet, since nothing's done by halves
While illusion's yet to do,
May we still forgive ourselves,
And dance again when trumpets blow.

VILLA ADRIANA

When the colossus of the will's dominion
Wavers and shrinks upon a dying eye,
Enormous shadows sit like birds of prey,
Waiting to fall where blistered marbles lie.

But in its open pools the place already
Lay ruined, before the old king left it free.
Shattered in waters of each marble basin
He might have seen it as today we see.

Dying in discontent, he must have known
How, once mere consciousness had turned its back,
The frescoes of his appetite would crumble,
The fountains of his longing yawn and crack.

And all his genius would become a riddle,
His perfect colonnades at last attain
The incompleteness of a natural thing;
His impulse turn to mystery again.

Who sleeps, and dreams, and wakes, and sleeps again
May dream again; so in the end we come
Back to the cherished and consuming scene
As if for once the stones will not be dumb.

We come like dreamers searching for an answer,
Passionately in need to reconstruct
The columned roofs under the blazing sky,
The courts so open, so forever locked.

And some of us, as dreamers, excavate
Under the blanching light of sleep's high noon,
The artifacts of thought, the site of love,
Whose Hadrian has given the slip, and gone.

THE EXPLORERS

Beside the Mare Crisium, that sea
Where water never was, sit down with me,
And let us talk of Earth, where long ago
We drank the air and saw the rivers flow
Like comets through the green estates of man,
And fruit the colour of Aldebaran
Weighted the curving boughs. The route of stars
Was our diversion, and the fate of Mars
Our grave concern; we stared throughout the night
On these uncolonized demesnes of light.
We read of stars escaping Newton's chain
Till only autographs of fire remain;
We aimed our mortal searchlights into space
As if in hopes to find a mortal face.

O little Earth, our village, where the day
Seemed all too brief, and starlight would not stay,
We were provincials on the grand express
That whirled us into dark and loneliness.
We thought to bring you wonder with a tale
Huger than those that turned our fathers pale.
Here in this lunar night we watch alone
Longer than ever men have watched for dawn.
Beyond this meteor-bitten plain we see
More starry systems than you dream to be,
And while their clockwork blazes overhead,
We speak the names we learned as we were bred,
We tell of places seen each day from birth—
Obscure and local, patois of the Earth!
O race of farmers, plowing year by year
The same few fields, I sometimes seem to hear

The far-off echo of a cattle-bell
Against the cratered cliff of Arzachel,
And weep to think no sound can ever come
Across that outer desert, from my home.

LANDSCAPE OF THE STAR

The silence of the year. This hour the streets
Lie empty, and the clash of bells is scattered
Out to the edge of stars. I heard them tell
Morning's first change and clang the people home
From crèche and scented aisle. Come home, come home,
I heard the bells of Christmas call and die.

This Christmas morning, in the stony streets
Of an unaccustomed city, where the gas
Quivers against the darkly-shuttered walls,
I walk, my breath a veil upon the cold,
No longer sick for home nor hunted down
By faces loved, by gate or sill or tree
That once I used to wreathe in red and silver
Under the splintered incense of the fir.

I think of those inscrutables who toiled,
Heavy and brooding in their camel-train,
Across the blue-wrapped stretches. Home behind,
Kingdoms departed from, the solemn journey
Their only residence: the starlit hour,
The landscape of the star, their time and place.

O to be one of them, and feel the sway
Of rocking camel through the Judaean sand,—
Ride, wrapped in swathes of damask and of silk,
Hear the faint ring of jewel in silver mesh
Starring the silence of the plain; and hold
With rigid fingers curved as in oblation
The golden jar of myrrh against the knees.

To ride thus, bearing gifts to a strange land,
To a strange King; nor think of fear and envy,

Being so bemused by starlight of one star,
The long unbroken journey, that all questions
Sink like the lesser lights behind the hills;
Think neither of the end in sight, nor all
That lies behind, but dreamlessly to ride,
Traveller at one with travelled countryside.

How else, since for those Magi and their train
The palaces behind have ceased to be
Home, and the home they travel toward is still
But rumor stoking fear in Herod's brain?
What else for them but this, since never more
Can courts and states receive them as they were,
Nor have the trampled earth, the roof of straw
Received the kings as they are yet to be?

The bells are silent, silenced in my mind
As on the dark. I walk, a foreigner,
Upon this night that calls all travellers home,
The prodigal forgiven, and the breach
Mended for this one feast. Yet all are strange
To their own ends, and their beginnings now
Cannot contain them. Once-familiar speech
Babbles in wayward dialect of a dream.

Our gifts shall bring us home: not to beginnings
Nor always to the destination named
Upon our setting-forth. Our gifts compel,
Master our ways and lead us in the end
Where we are most ourselves; whether at last
To Solomon's gaze or Sheba's silken knees
Or winter pastures underneath a star,
Where angels spring like starlight in the trees.

LETTER FROM THE LAND
OF SINNERS

I write you this out of another province
That you may never see:
Country of rivers, its topography
Mutable in detail, yet always one,
Blasted in certain places, here by glaciers,
There by the work of man.

The fishers by the water have no boast
Save of their freedom; here
A man may cast a dozen kinds of lure
And think his days rewarded if he sight
Now and again the prize, unnetted, flicking
Its prism-gleams of light.

The old lord lived secluded in his park
Until the hall was burned
Years ago, by his tenants; both have learned
Better since then, and now our children run
To greet him. Quail and hunter have forgotten
The echo of the gun.

I said there are blasted places: we have kept
Their nakedness intact—
No marble to commemorate an act
Superhuman or merely rash; we know
Why they are there and why the seed that falls there
Is certain not to grow.

We keep these places as we keep the time
Scarred on our recollection
When some we loved broke from us in defection,
Or we ourselves harried to death too soon
What we could least forgo. Our memories
Recur like the old moon.

But we have made another kind of peace,
And walk where boughs are green,
Forgiven by the selves that we have been,
And learning to forgive. Our apples taste
Sweeter this year; our gates are falling down,
And need not be replaced.

CONCORD RIVER

The turtles on the ledges of July
Heard our approach and splashed. Now in the mud
Lie like the memory of fecund summer
Their buried eggs. The river, colder now,
Has other, autumn tales to carry on
Between the banks where lovers used to lie.

Lovers, or boys escaped from yard and farm
To drown in sensual purities of sun—
No matter which; for single fisherman
Casting into the shade, or those absorbed
In human ardor, summer was the same,
Impervious to weariness or alarm.

The fisherman, by craft and love removed
From meanness, has an almanac at home
Saying the season will be brief this year
And ice strike early; yet upon its shelf
The book is no despoiler of this day
In which he moves and ponders, most himself.

That boy, watching for turtles by the shore,
Steeped in his satisfactory loneliness,
If asked could tell us that the sun would set,
Or autumn drive him back to games and school—
Tell us at second-hand, believing then
Only midsummer and the noonstruck pool.

And we, who floated through the sunlit green,
Indolent, voluntary as the dance
Of dragon-flies above the skimming leaves—
For us the landscape and the hour became
A single element, where our drifting silence
Fell twofold, like our shadows on the water.

This is the Concord River, where the ice
Will hold till April: this is the willowed stream
Much threaded by the native cogitators
Who wrote their journals calmly by its shore,
Observing weather and the swing of seasons
Along with personal cosmologies.

Henry Thoreau most nearly learned to live
Within a world his soul could recognize—
Unshaken by accounts of any country
He could not touch with both his hands. He saw
The river moving past the provincial town
And knew each curve of shoreline for his own.

He travelled much, he said—his wayward speech
Sounding always a little insolent,
Yet surer than the rest; they, like ourselves,
Ran off to dabble in a world beyond,
While he exalted the geography
He lived each day: a river and a pond.

For him there was no turning of the ear
To rumored urgencies that sought to rouse
The fisher from his pool, the serious child
From his unconscious wandering: the sound
Of desperate enterprises rang to him
Fictive as ghosts upon old Indian ground.

Lover and child and fisherman, alike
Have in their time been native to this shore
As he would have it peopled: all entranced
By such concerns in their perfected hour
That in their lives the river and the tree
Are absolutes, no longer scenery.

APOLOGY

You, invincibly yourself,
Have nothing left to say.
The stones upon the mountainside
Are not more free,
Bearing all question, all reproach
Without reply.

The dead, who keep their peace intact,
Although they know
Much we might be gainers by,
Are proud like you—
Or, if they spoke, might sound as you
Sounded just now.

For every angry, simple man
The word is but
A shadow, and his motive grows
More still and great
While the world hums around him, wild
That he should explicate.

And Socrates, whose crystal tongue
Perturbs us now,
Left all unsatisfied; the word
Can never show
Reason enough for what a man
Knows he must do.

You told us little, and are done.
So might the dead
Begin to speak of dying, then
Leave half unsaid.
Silence like thunder bears its own
Excuse for dread.

LIVING IN SIN

She had thought the studio would keep itself;
no dust upon the furniture of love.
Half heresy, to wish the taps less vocal,
the panes relieved of grime. A plate of pears,
a piano with a Persian shawl, a cat
stalking the picturesque amusing mouse
had risen at his urging.
Not that at five each separate stair would writhe
under the milkman's tramp; that morning light
so coldly would delineate the scraps
of last night's cheese and three sepulchral bottles;
that on the kitchen shelf among the saucers
a pair of beetle-eyes would fix her own—
envoy from some village in the moldings . . .
Meanwhile, he, with a yawn,
sounded a dozen notes upon the keyboard,
declared it out of tune, shrugged at the mirror,
rubbed at his beard, went out for cigarettes;
while she, jeered by the minor demons,
pulled back the sheets and made the bed and found
a towel to dust the table-top,
and let the coffee-pot boil over on the stove.
By evening she was back in love again,
though not so wholly but throughout the night
she woke sometimes to feel the daylight coming
like a relentless milkman up the stairs.

AUTUMN EQUINOX

The leaves that shifted overhead all summer
Are marked for earth now, and I bring the baskets
Still dark with clingings of another season
Up from the cellar. All the house is still,
Now that I've left it. Lyman in his study
Peers on a page of Dryden by the window,
Eyes alone moving, like a mended quaint
Piece of old clockwork. When the afternoon
Trails into half-light, he will never notice
Until I come indoors to light the lamps
And rouse him blinking from the brownish type,
The gilt and tarnished spine of volume five
Out of the glass-doored cabinet in the hall.
Why Satires, I have wondered? For I've seen
The title-page, and riffled through the volume,
When he was gone. I thought that growing old
Returned one to a vague Arcadian longing,
To Ovid, Spenser, something golden-aged,
Some incorruptible myth that tinged the years
With pastoral flavours. Lyman, too, as gentle
As an old shepherd, half-apologetic
When I come bustling to disturb his dreams—
What in that bitterness can speak to him
Or help him down these final sloping decades
With kindly arm? I've never been a scholar—
Reader, perhaps at times, but not a scholar,
Not in the way that Lyman used to be—
And yet I know there's acid on the page
He pores—that least acidulous of men.
While I, who spent my youth and middle-age
In stubbornness and railing, pass the time
Now, after fifty, raking in the sun
The leaves that sprinkle slowly on the grass,

And feel their gold like firelight at my back,
In slow preoccupation with September.

Sometimes I call across to Alice Hume
And meet her at the fence as women meet
To say the weather's seasonably fine,
Talk husbands, bargains, or philosophize—
The dry philosophy of neighborhood.
She thinks perhaps how sharp of tongue and quick
I used to be, and how I've quieted down,
Without those airs because I'd married Lyman,
Professor at the college, while her husband
Was just another farmer. That was pride
As raw and silly as the girl I was—
Reading too much, sneering at other girls
Whose learning was of cookery and flirtation.
Father would have me clever, sometimes said
He'd let me train for medicine, like a son,
To come into his practice. So I studied
German and botany, and hated both.
What good for me to know the Latin name
For huckleberry, while the others climbed
To pick the fruit and kissed across the bushes?
I never was a scholar, but I had
A woman's love for men of intellect,
A woman's need for love of any kind.

So Lyman came to ask me of my father:
Stiff-collared, shy, not quite the man I'd dreamed—
(Byron and Matthew Arnold vaguely mingled
Without the disadvantages of either.)
And yet he seemed superb in his refusal
To read aloud from Bryant to the ladies
Assembled on the boarding-house piazza
Among the moth-wings of a summer evening.
His quick withdrawal won my heart. I smile

Sometimes to think what quirks of vanity
Propel us toward our choices in the end.

The wedding-picture in the bureau drawer
Has on the back in Lyman's measured writing:
"September twenty-second, nineteen-twelve."
I keep it in its folder, deckle-edged
And yellowing. I see myself again,
Correct and terrified on our wedding-day,
Wearing the lace my mother wore before me
And buttoned shoes that pinched. I feel again
The trembling of my hand in Lyman's fingers,
Awkwardly held in that ungainly pose
While aunts around us nodded like the Fates
That nemesis was accomplished. Lyman stood
So thin and ministerial in his black,
I thought he looked a stranger. In the picture
We are the semblance of a bride and groom
Static as figures on a mantelpiece,
As if that moment out of time existed
Then and forever in a dome of glass,
Where neither dust nor the exploring fly
Could speck its dry immutability.

Thus I became his partner in a life
Annual, academic; we observed
Events momentous as the ceremony
To dedicate the chapel carillon
(Memorial to Edward Stephens Hodge,
Class of nineteen-fourteen). There we heard
Those sounds converge upon the rural air
That soon became familiar as a hinge
Creaking and never silenced. In our meadow
The angular young took up their bats and shouted
Throughout the afternoon, while I was pouring
Tea for the dean's arthritic wife. For Lyman

The world was all the distance he pursued
From home to lecture-room, and home again,
Exchanging nods with colleagues, smiling vaguely
Upon a shirtsleeved trio, tanned and jostling,
Who grinned and gave him room upon the path.
I bit my fingers, changed the parlor curtains
To ones the like of which were never seen
Along our grave and academic street.
I brought them home from Springfield in a bundle
And hung them in defiance. I took a walk
Across the fields one heavy summer night
Until the college from a mile away
Looked sallow, insignificant in the moonlight.
It seemed the moon must shine on finer things
I had not seen, things that could show with pride
Beneath that silver globe. Along the walls
Of Lyman's study there were steel engravings
Framed in black oak: the crazy tower of Pisa,
The Pyramids, rooted in desert sand,
Cologne Cathedral with its dangerous spires
Piercing the atmosphere. I hated them
For priggishly enclosing in a room
The marvels of the world, as if declaring
Such was the right and fitting rôle of marvels.

Night, and I wept aloud; half in my sleep,
Half feeling Lyman's wonder as he leaned
Above to shake me. "Are you ill, unhappy?
Tell me what I can do."
　　　　　　　　"I'm sick, I guess—
I thought that life was different than it is."

"Tell me what's wrong. Why can't you ever say?
I'm here, you know."
                              Half shamed, I turned to see
The lines of grievous love upon his face,
The love that gropes and cannot understand.
"I must be crazy, Lyman—or a dream
Has made me babble things I never thought.
Go back to sleep—I won't be so again."

Young lovers talk of giving all the heart
Into each others' trust: their rhetoric
Won't stand for analyzing, I'm aware,
But have they thought of this: that each must know
Beyond a doubt what's given, what received?

Now we are old like Nature; patient, staid,
Unhurried from the year's wellworn routine,
We wake and take the day for what it is,
And sleep as calmly as the dead who know
They'll wake to their reward. We have become
As unselfconscious as a pair of trees,
Not questioning, but living. Even autumn
Can only carry through what spring began.
What else could happen now but loss of leaf
And rain upon the boughs? So I have thought,
And wondered faintly where the thought began,
And when the irritable gust of youth
Stopped turning every blade of grass to find
A new dissatisfaction. Meanwhile Lyman
Reads satire in the falling afternoon—
A change for him as well. We finish off
Not quite as we began. I hear the bells
Wandering through the air across the fields.
I've raked three bushel baskets full of leaves—
Enough for one September afternoon.

THE STRAYED VILLAGE

He had come nearly half a thousand miles,
And then to find it gone . . . He knew too well
Ever to be mistaken, where the hills
Dipped to reveal it first: the line of chimneys
Reflected in the unimportant stream,
The monument, worth half a line in guidebooks—
"Tower of a church that Cromwell's army burned,
Fine early Perpendicular"—itself
Subservient neither to theologies
Nor changing styles of architecture, still
A cipher on the landscape, something clear
In that unostentatious scenery.

Well, if the tower was gone—and who should say,
Depend on any landmark to remain?
He had been too far and known too many losses
Not to be reconciled that even landmarks
Go out like matches when you need them most.
So it could be with this. But not a house,
Not anything reflected in the river
But willows that could grow by any river,
Feminine, non-committal in their postures.
Willows: a bridge then? But the bridge was gone,
The piles had left no trace, no signature
Of stones beside the water. If, indeed,
There ever had been bridge or tower or house.
That was the question that enforeigned him,
Brushed forty years of memory aside
And made of him another obtuse tripper
Staring at signposts to be reassured:
This *is* the place—where I grew into manhood,
The place I had to leave when I was grown?

So often he had thought a man's whole life
Most rightly could be written, like his own,
In terms of places he was forced to leave
Because their meaning, passing that of persons,
Became too much for him.
                                 "This *is* the place?"
He heard himself demand; and heard the other—
A youthful rector, by the look of him,
Pausing upon his evening stroll—reply,
"Oh, yes, this is the *place*. . . . The village went,
As I should reckon, twenty years ago.
Across the hill, in our town, there was once
Talk and conjecture; now you might suppose
Only the antiquarians breathe its name.
The memory of man, my friend, is short."
"Shorter and longer than it's credited,"
He answered; "but you say the village went?
I hardly care to ask, and yet I ask—
By flood? by fire? There used to be a tower
That Cromwell's zealots failed to bully down.
But there's no mark. It *went?* How did it go?"

"It went away. You've heard of men who went,
Suddenly, without partings or annulments,
Not carried off by accident or death,
But simply strayed? That was the way it went.
We went to bed on Thursday and could hear
The bells, as usual on a quiet night,
Across the hill between. On Friday morning
There were no bells. There wasn't anything.
The landscape stood as if since Magna Carta,
Empty, as it stands now. The village had gone,
Quite without taking leave. Strayed, is the word
We found ourselves as if by acquiescence
Using to speak of it, as if we thought
Someday to come upon it somewhere else

And greet our former neighbors as before.
No one has ever found it, though. One can't
Advertise for a village that has strayed:
'Lost, with one early Perpendicular tower,
A village numbering four hundred souls,
With stone and wooden footbridge.' And, as I say,
Men's memories grow short like winter daylight.
So much gets strayed that has to be replaced—
Dogs, wits, affections . . ."
                                         "Yes, so much gets strayed;
But one of all the things a man can lose
I thought would keep till I could come again.
It almost seems it went lest I should come,
Because I always promised I would come,
And had this latest penalty in store,
The last of losses."

                                         So he said goodbye,
And watched the little rector climb the hill
Back to his parish town. The stream ran on,
And all that walking was to do again.

THE PERENNIAL ANSWER

The way the world came swinging round my ears
I knew what Doctor meant the day he said,
"Take care, unless you want to join your dead;
It's time to end this battling with your years."
He knew I'd have the blackest word told straight,
Whether it was my child that couldn't live,
Or Joel's mind, thick-riddled like a sieve
With all that loving festered into hate.
Better to know the ways you are accurst,
And stand up fierce and glad to hear the worst.
The blood is charged, the back is stiffened so.

Well, on that day that was a day ago,
And yet so many hours and years ago
Numbered in seizures of a darkening brain,
I started up the attic stairs again—
The fifth time in the hour—not thinking then
That it was hot, but knowing the air sat stiller
Under the eaves than when the idiot killer
Hid in the Matthews barn among the hay
And all the neighbors through one August day
Waited outside with pitchforks in the sun.
Joel waited too, and when they heard the gun
Resound so flatly in the loft above
He was the one to give the door a shove
And climb the ladder. A man not made for love,
But built for things of violence; he would stand
Where lightning flashed and watch with eyes so wide
You thought the prongs of fire would strike inside;
Or sit with some decaying book in hand,
Reading of spirits and the evil-eyed,
And witches' sabbaths in a poisoned land.

So it was Joel that brought the fellow out,
Tarnished with hay and blood. I still can see
The eyes that Joel turned and fixed on me
When it was done—as if by rights his wife
Should go to him for having risked his life
And say—I hardly knew what thing he wanted.
I know it was a thing I never granted,
And what his mind became, from all that woe,
Those violent concerns he lived among,
Was on my head as well. I couldn't go,
I never went to him, I never clung
One moment on his breast. But I was young.

And I was cruel, a girl-bride seeing only
Her marriage as a room so strange and lonely
She looked outside for warmth. And in what fashion
Could I be vessel for that sombre passion—
For Joel, decreed till death to have me all?
The tortured grandsire hanging in the hall
Depicted by a limner's crabbed hand
Seemed more a being that I could understand.
How could I help but look beyond that wall
And probe the lawful stones that built it strong
With questions sharper than a pitchfork's prong?
If Joel knew, he kept his silence long.

But Evans and I were hopeless from the start:
He, collared early by a rigorous creed,
Not man of men but man of God indeed,
Whose eye had seen damnation, and whose heart
Thrust all it knew of passion into one
Chamber of iron inscribed *Thy will be done.*
Yet sense will have revenge on one who tries
To down his senses with the brand of lies.

The road was empty from the village home,
Empty of all but us and that dark third,
The sudden Northern spring. There must be some
For whom the thrusting blood, so long deferred
In alder-stem and elm, is not the rise
Of flood in their own veins; some who can see
That green unholy dance without surprise.
I only say it has been this for me:
The time of thinnest ice, of casualty
More swift and deadly than the skater's danger.
The end of March could make me stand a stranger
On my own doorstep, and the daily shapes
Of teapot, ladle, or the china grapes
I kept in winter on the dresser shelf
Rebuked me, made me foreign to myself.

Evans beside me on that moonless road
Walked hard as if he thought behind us strode
Pursuers he had fled through weary ways.
He only said: "Where I was born and grew,
You felt the spring come on you like a daze
Slow out of February, and you knew
The thing you were contending with. But here—"

"Spring is a bolt of lightning on the year,"
I said, "it strikes before you feel it near."

"The change of seasons is another thing
God put on earth to try us, I believe.
As if the breaking-out of green could bring
Escape from frozen discipline, give us leave
To taste of things by will and law forbidden."

"Maybe it was the weather lost us Eden,"
I said, but faltering, and the words went by
Like flights of moths under that star-soaked sky.

And that was all. He brought me to the door;
The house was dark, but on the upper floor
A light burned in the hallway. "Joel's asleep,"
I told him, and put out my hand. His touch
Was cold as candles kept unlit in church,
And yet I felt his seeking fingers creep
About my wrist and seize it in their grip
Until they hurt me.
                   "Neither you nor I
Have lived in Eden, but they say we die
To gain that day at last. We have to live
Believing it—what else can we believe?"

"Why not believe in life?" I said, but heard
Only the sanctioned automatic word
"Eternal life—" perennial answer given
To those who ask on earth a taste of heaven.

The penalty you pay for dying last
Is facing those transactions from the past
That would detain you when you try to go.
All night last night I lay and seemed to hear
The to-and-fro of callers down below,
Even the knocker rattling on the door.
I thought the dead had heard my time was near
To meet them, and had come to tell me so;
But not a footstep sounded on the stair.
If they are gone it means a few days more
Are left, or they would wait. Joel would wait
Down by the dark old clock that told me late
That night from Boston. "Evans walked me home;
We sat together in the train by chance."
But not a word; only his burning glance.
"We stopped to have some coffee in the station.
Why do you stand like that? What if I come
An hour or so after the time I said?

The house all dark, I thought you'd gone to bed."
But still that gaze, not anger, indignation,
Nor anything so easy, but a look
As fixed as when he stared upon his book.
No matter if my tale was false or true,
I was a woodcut figure on the page,
On trial for a nameless sin. Then rage
Took him like fire where lightning dives. I knew
That he could kill me then, but what he did
Was wrench me up the stairs, onto the bed.

The night of Joel's death I slept alone
In this same room. A neighbor said she'd stay,
Thinking the dead man lying down below
Might keep the living from rest. She told me so:
"Those hours before the dawn can lie like stone
Upon the heart—I've lain awake—I know."
At last I had to take the only way,
And said, "The nights he was alive and walking
From room to room and hearing spirits talking,
What sleep I had was likelier to be broken."
Her face was shocked but I was glad I'd spoken.
"Well, if you feel so—" She would tell the tale
Next morning, but at last I was alone
In an existence finally my own.

And yet I knew that Evans would find reason
Why we were not our own, nor had our will
Unhindered; that disturbance of a season
So long removed was something he would kill
Yet, if he had not killed it. When I stood
Beside the churchyard fence and felt his glance
Reluctantly compelling mine, the blood
Soared to my face, the tombstones seemed to dance
Dizzily, till I turned. The eyes I met
Accused as they implored me to forget,

As if my shape had risen to destroy
Salvation's rampart with a hope of joy.
My lips betrayed their *Why?* but then his face
Turned from me, and I saw him leave the place.
Now Joel and Evans are neighbors, down beneath.

I wonder what we're bound to after death?
I wonder what's exacted of the dead,
How many debts of conscience still are good?
Not Evans or his Bible ever said
That spirit must complete what flesh and blood
Contracted in their term. What creditors
Will wait and knock for us at marble doors?

I'd like to know which stays when life is past:
The marriage kept in fear, the love deferred,
The footstep waited for and never heard,
The pressure of five fingers round the wrist
Stopping its beat with pain, the mouth unkissed,
The dream whose waking startles into sight
A figure mumbling by the bed at night,
The hopeless promise of eternal life—
Take now your Scripture, Evans, if you will,
And see how flimsily the pages spill
From spines reduced to dust. What have they said
Of us, to what will they pronounce me wife?
My debt is paid: the rest is on your head.

THE INSOMNIACS

The mystic finishes in time,
The actor finds himself in space;
And each, wherever he has been,
Must know his hand before his face,
Must crawl back into his own skin
As in the darkness after crime
The thief can hear his breath again,
Resume the knowledge of his limbs
And how the spasm goes and comes
Under the bones that cage his heart.

So: we are fairly met, grave friend—
The meeting of two wounds in man.
I, gesturing with practised hand,
I, in my great brocaded gown,
And you, the fixed and patient one,
Enduring all the world can do.
I, with my shifting masks, the gold,
The awful scarlet, laughing blue,
Maker of many worlds; and you,
Worldless, the pure receptacle.

And yet your floating eyes reveal
What saint or mummer groans to feel:
That finite creatures finally know
The damp of stone beneath the knees,
The stiffness in the folded hands
A duller ache than holy wounds,
The draught that never stirs the sleeve
Of glazed evangelists above,
But drives men out from sacred calm
Into the violent, wayward sun.

My voice commands the formal stage;
A jungle thrives beyond the wings—
All formless and benighted things
That rhetoric cannot assuage.
I speak a dream and turn to see
The sleepness night outstaring me.
My pillow sweats; I wake in space.
This is my hand before my face.
This is the headboard of my bed
Whose splinters stuff my nightmare mouth;

This is the unconquerable drouth
I carry in my burning head.
Not my words nor your visions mend
Such infamous knowledge. We are split,
Done into bits, undone, pale friend,
As ecstasy begets its end;
As we are spun of rawest thread—
The flaw is in us; we will break.
O dare you of this fracture make
Hosannas plain and tragical,

Or dare I let each cadence fall
Awkward as learning newly learned,
Simple as children's cradle songs,
As untranslatable and true,
We someday might conceive a way
To do the thing we long to do—
To do what men have always done—
To live in time, to act in space
Yet find a ritual to embrace
Raw towns of man, the pockmarked sun.

THE SNOW QUEEN

Child with a chip of mirror in his eye
Saw the world ugly, fled to plains of ice
Where beauty was the Snow Queen's promises.
Under my lids a splinter sharp as his
Has made me wish you lying dead
Whose image digs the needle deeper still.

In the deceptive province of my birth
I had seen yes turn no, the saints descend,
Their sacred faces twisted into smiles,
The stars gone lechering, the village spring
Gush mud and toads—all miracles
Befitting an incalculable age.

To love a human face was to discover
The cracks of paint and varnish on the brow;
Soon to distrust all impulses of flesh
That strews its sawdust on the chamber floor,
While at the window peer two crones
Who once were Juliet and Jessica.

No matter, since I kept a little while
One thing intact from that perversity—
Though landscapes bloomed in monstrous cubes and coils.
In you belonged simplicities of light
To mend distraction, teach the air
To shine, the stars to find their way again.

Yet here the Snow Queen's cold prodigious will
Commands me, and your face has lost its power,
Dissolving to its opposite like the rest.
Under my ribs a diamond splinter now
Sticks, and has taken root; I know
Only this frozen spear that drives me through.

LOVE IN THE MUSEUM

Now will you stand for me, in this cool light,
Infanta reared in ancient etiquette,
A point-lace queen of manners. At your feet
The doll-like royal dog demurely set
Upon a chequered floor of black and white.

Or be a Louis' mistress, by Boucher,
Lounging on cushions, silken feet asprawl
Upon a couch where casual cupids play
While on your arms and shoulders seems to fall
The tired extravagance of a sunset day.

Or let me think I pause beside a door
And see you in a bodice by Vermeer,
Where light falls quartered on the polished floor
And rims the line of water tilting clear
Out of an earthen pitcher as you pour.

But art requires a distance: let me be
Always the connoisseur of your perfection.
Stay where the spaces of the gallery
Flow calm between your pose and my inspection,
Lest one imperfect gesture make demands
As troubling as the touch of human hands.

I HEARD A HERMIT SPEAK

Upon the mountain of the young
I heard a hermit speak:
"Purity is the serpent's eye
That murders with a look.

Purity's king of poisons
And duke of deadly night.
Abhor the single-minded man,
The woman lily-white.

Go cold under the heavens,
Run naked through the day,
But never wear the armored shirt
Of total Yea or Nay.

Stare into the looking-glass:
Your enemy stares you back.
Yet never cringe and hide your face;
Hear all that he will speak.

The day that glass dissolves to show
Your own reflection there,
Then change your mirror for the world,
The teeming, streaming air.

O let your human memory end
Heavy with thought and act.
Claim every joy of paradox
That time would keep intact.

Be rich as you are human,"
I heard that hermit cry
To the young men and women
All walking out to die.

COLOPHON

In this long room, upon each western pane
The sunset wreaks its final savage stain;
And we, like masquers costumed in an air
Outcrimsoning the gaudiest cock that crows,
Parade as torches and diabolos
Along the blood-red spiral of the stair.

An imminent amazement of the heart
Constricts our greetings as we meet and part.
A gesture or a word can make us turn
Ready to cry a sudden sharp goodnight;
Yet still delays the dark, still cockerel-bright
Smoulder the dyes in which we wade and burn.

Not tragical, the faces that we wear:
A modern gaiety, fitting as despair
Shall pass the hour till domes and sunsets fall.
Extravagant and ceremonious words
Rise on the air like flights of Chinese birds
Uncaged upon a fiery carnival.

What's left us in this violent spectacle
But kisses on the mouth, or works of will—
The imagination's form so sternly wrought,
The flashes of the brain so boldly penned
That when the sunset gutters to its end
The world's last thought will be our flaring thought?

A WALK BY THE CHARLES

Finality broods upon the things that pass:
Persuaded by this air, the trump of doom
Might hang unsounded while the autumn gloom
Darkens the leaf and smokes the river's glass.
For nothing so susceptible to death
But on this forenoon seems to hold its breath:
The silent single oarsmen on the stream
Are always young, are rowers in a dream.
The lovers underneath the chestnut tree,
Though love is over, stand bemused to see
The season falling where no fall could be.

You oarsmen, when you row beyond the bend,
Will see the river winding to its end.
Lovers that hold the chestnut burr in hand
Will speak at last of death, will understand,
Foot-deep amid the ruinage of the year,
What smell it is that stings the gathering air.

From our evasions we are brought at last,
From all our hopes of constancy, to cast
One look of recognition at the sky,
The unimportant leaves that flutter by.
Why else upon this bank are we so still?
What lends us anchor but the mutable?

O lovers, let the bridge of your two hands
Be broken, like the mirrored bridge that bends
And shivers on the surface of the stream.
Young oarsmen, who in timeless gesture seem
Continuous, united with the tide,
Leave off your bending to the oar, and glide
Past innocence, beyond these aging bricks
To where the Charles flows in to join the Styx.

NEW YEAR MORNING

The bells have quit their clanging; here beneath
The coldly furious streaks of morning stars
We hear the scraping of the last few cars,
And on the doorstep by the frozen wreath
Return goodnights to night. Dear friends, once more
We've held our strength against a straining door,

Again the siege is past, another year
Has lost the battle. You can leave us now.
The hours are done that must be clamored through
Lest darkness think us sleeping, lest we hear
Secret police engendered out of night
Advancing on our little zone of light.

Now each of us can dare to be alone,
His room no longer populous with spies
Bending above the pillow where he lies
To sow his dreams with fear that all is done,
That there's no more reprieve, no leaf to tear
And find another January there.

So we are safe again. Goodnight, brave friends.
So may beginnings always follow ends.
Though time is treasonable, may we stand
Gathered each year, a stubborn-hearted band
Whose gaiety rises like a litany
Under the dying ornamental tree.

IN TIME OF CARNIVAL

Those lights, that plaza—I should know them all:
The impotent blind beggar shouting his songs
Of lovers, while the headlong populace
Drinks, tramples, immolates itself in action;
The bloody light of braziers on the faces
Of women who are action's means and end,
Each a laughing Fury; the towering glass
Of those cathedral saints, whose stiffened forms,
Ruby in passing torchlight, stoop to dark
And flare again as puppets of disorder,
Lifeless without its light, but in that rout
Illumined and empowered. There's no crowd
In nave or playhouse any more; for all
Are actors where mere pasteboard roars to heaven
Under the dropped match, and the streets alone,
The amphitheatre of great night itself,
Suffice to contain their scene. Nothing will do
But action of the senses, total seizure
Of what's to hand. And through the swaying streets
That beggar, impotent since youth, sings on,
Ignorant of the scene, blind to his power,
The songs that send those lovers wild to bed.

THE MIDDLE-AGED

Their faces, safe as an interior
Of Holland tiles and Oriental carpet,
Where the fruit-bowl, always filled, stood in a light
Of placid afternoon—their voices' measure,
Their figures moving in the Sunday garden
To lay the tea outdoors or trim the borders,
Afflicted, haunted us. For to be young
Was always to live in other people's houses
Whose peace, if we sought it, had been made by others,
Was ours at second-hand and not for long.
The custom of the house, not ours, the sun
Fading the silver-blue Fortuny curtains,
The reminiscence of a Christmas party
Of fourteen years ago—all memory,
Signs of possession and of being possessed,
We tasted, tense with envy. They were so kind,
Would have given us anything; the bowl of fruit
Was filled for us, there was a room upstairs
We must call ours: but twenty years of living
They could not give. Nor did they ever speak
Of the coarse stain on that polished balustrade,
The crack in the study window, or the letters
Locked in a drawer and the key destroyed.
All to be understood by us, returning
Late, in our own time—how that peace was made,
Upon what terms, with how much left unsaid.

THE MARRIAGE PORTION

From commissars of daylight
Love cannot make us free.
Nights of ungracious darkness
Hang over you and me.
We lie awake together
And hear the clocks strike three.

Our loving cannot exile
The felons *but* and *if;*
Yet being undivided
Some ways we can contrive
To hold off those besiegers
Who batter round our life:

The thieves of our completeness
Who steal us stone by stone,
The patronage that scowls upon
Our need to be alone,
And all the clever people
Who want us for their own.

The telephone is ringing,
And planes and trains depart.
The cocktail party's forming,
The cruise about to start.
To stay behind is fatal—
Act now, the time is short.

If we refuse the summons
And stand at last alone,
We walk intact and certain,
As man and woman grown
In the deserted playground
When all the rest have gone.

THE TREE

Long ago I found a seed,
And kept it in a glass of water,
And half forgot my dim intent
Until I saw it start to reach
For life with one blind, fragile root.
And then I pressed it into earth
And saw its tendrils seek the air,
So slowly that I hardly knew
Of any change till it had grown
A stalk, a leaf; and seemed to be
No more a thing in need of me,
But living by some sapience
I had not given, could not withdraw.
So it grew on, and days went by,
And seasons with their common gifts,
Till at the leafage of the year
I felt the sun cut off from me
By something thick outside my room—
Not yet a tree grown to the full,
Yet so endowed with need and will
It took the warmth and left me cold.
And first I climbed with hook and shears
To prune the boughs that darkened me,
But the tree was stubborner than I,
And where I clipped it grew again,
Brutal in purpose as a weed.
Nor did it give of fruit or flower,
Though seasons brought their common gifts,
And years went by. It only grew
Darker and denser to my view,
Taking whatever I would yield—

The homage of a troubled mind—
Requiring nothing, yet accepting
My willingness to guard its life
By the endurance of my own.
It gives me nothing; yet I see
Sometimes in dreams my enemy
Hanged by the hair upon that tree.

LOVERS ARE LIKE CHILDREN

Chagall's sweet lovers mounting into blue
Remind me that discovery by two
Of any world the mind can wander through

Is like the time when young and left alone,
We touched the secret fringe of being one,
Back of the playground full of Everyone.

Love is like childhood, caught in trust and fear.
The statues point to omens in the air,
And yet the fountains bubble bright and clear.

Lost in the garden rank with contradiction,
We see the fences sprout for our affliction,
And the red-rose-tree curtly labelled Fiction.

Nothing to tell us whether what they mean
Is true of this or any other scene.
We only know the summer leaves are green,

Alive and dense for two to penetrate—
An exploration difficult and great
As when one day beside the schoolyard gate,

Straggling behind to glean a sunlit stone,
One first perceived and knew itself as one.
Now add this pebble to that early one.

WHEN THIS CLANGOR
IN THE BRAIN

Say a master of the track
Lightly leaped and lightly ran,
Knew his powers of chest and thigh
Clean outstripped the thought of man—
Would it not be pill and patch
And worse than queasy cripples know,
If on a day the rheum should catch
And lay that master leaper low?

Say that into certain minds
A Merlin dances, in and out,
And what he chooses, must obey
And sway the thought it thinks about—
Would it not be old folks' home
And the dry end of the year
For the mind he left again
Unmastered, lock and stock and gear?

When this clangor in the brain
Grows perfunctory, or worse,
Put me down a sick old woman
Propped for sleep, hire me a nurse;
Till then, all things I look upon
Beat on my brain to hail and bless,
And every last and wayward power
I claim till then, and nothing less.

A VIEW OF MERTON COLLEGE

An interval: the view across the fields
Perfect and insusceptible as seen
In printshops of the High Street—sun on stone
Worn like old needlework, the sheen of grass,
Minute and ageless figures moving down
The Broad Walk under tinted trees. Awhile
Mind's local jangling lightens, ear is eased,
Eye's flaw is mended in such gazing, healed
By separation as through glass. Until
Sun shifts, air turns harsher, paler, rooks
Flap in the rising wind. The wind has found you,
The mortal light of day, whose envy, waste,
Irresolution tread you as you go
Guilty and human. Here as anywhere,
Peace of the mind lies through an arch of stone,
The limitations posted strict and clear:
Not to be littered or presumed upon.

HOLIDAY

Summer was another country, where the birds
Woke us at dawn among the dripping leaves
And lent to all our fêtes their sweet approval.
The touch of air on flesh was lighter, keener,
The senses flourished like a laden tree
Whose every gesture finishes in a flower.
In those unwardened provinces we dined
From wicker baskets by a green canal,
Staining our lips with peach and nectarine,
Slapping at golden wasps. And when we kissed,
Tasting that sunlit juice, the landscape folded
Into our clasp, and not a breath recalled
The long walk back to winter, leagues away.

THE CAPITAL

Under that summer asphalt, under vistas
Aspiring to a neo-classic calm,
The steaming burgeon of Potomac's swamp
Has never quite been laid to rest. The eye
Winces in sunlight off a marble dome.

But cannot fix the face of Jefferson
Through haze of an outrageous atmosphere
By diplomats called tropic; nor can the ear
Hold to the lifeline of a single voice
Through jettisoned rumors jamming all the air.

The dollar in that city of inscriptions
Is minted among pediments and columns
Purer than newmade coin. The afternoon
Steams with the drip of departmental fountains
And humid branches breathing overhead

Down avenues where the siren's nervous shriek
Pursues the murderer or the foreign guest
Through those indifferent noonday crowds who never
Ask, till history tells them, what they do
In that metropolis anything but Greek.

THE PLATFORM

The railway stations of our daily plight
See every hour love's threatened overthrow.
Each afternoon at five the buses go
Laden with those who shall be false by night.
We say goodbye in rooms too bright with noise
To catch the shades of a receding voice;
We turn at the revolving door and see
Love's face already changed, indelibly.

Not to admit we may not meet again—
This was the parting treason of our thought.
Battering down our cowardly "till then,"
Time's traffic hems the seeker from the sought.
We take too sudden leave; the platform reels
With thunder of a thousand pounding heels,
And at the gate where one remains behind,
Though most we strain to see, we most are blind.

Dear loves, dear friends, I take my leave all day
In practice for a time that need not come.
I turn and move from you a little way,
As men walk out beyond the fields of home
In troubled days, to view what they love well—
Distance confirming for a moment's spell,
Meeting or going, that when we embrace
We know the heart beyond the transient face.

LAST SONG

All in the day that I was born,
I walked across the shouting corn;
I saw the sunlight flash and hail
From every spire and every sail,
But most I leaned against the sky
To hear the eagles racing by,
And all the safety of the womb
Could not betray me, lure me home.

All in the day that I was wed
I saw them strew my bridal bed.
I smelled the wind across the sheets
Breathing of lavender and sweets
That neither sea nor meadow knew;
And when my bride was brought to view
I kept a hundred candles lit
All for light and the joy of it.

All in the day that I was old
I felt the wind blow salt and cold
Like seaspray on my shaking thighs
Or sand flung up to blind my eyes.
I cried for sun and the eagles flying,
But felt those fingers spying, prying,
The same that wrenched me into life
And cut my safety with a knife.

Soon they will bind me dark and warm
And impotent to suffer harm.
I shall be exiled to the womb
Where once I lay and thought it home.
The sun that flashed my first delight
Shall never learn to cleave that night;
And all the swords of danger fly
Far from the caul in which I lie.

THE DIAMOND CUTTERS

However legendary,
The stone is still a stone,
Though it had once resisted
The weight of Africa,
The hammer-blows of time
That wear to bits of rubble
The mountain and the pebble—
But not this coldest one.

Now, you intelligence
So late dredged up from dark
Upon whose smoky walls
Bison took fumbling form
Or flint was edged on flint—
Now, careful arriviste,
Delineate at will
Incisions in the ice.

Be serious, because
The stone may have contempt
For too-familiar hands,
And because all you do
Loses or gains by this:
Respect the adversary,
Meet it with tools refined,
And thereby set your price.

Be hard of heart, because
The stone must leave your hand.
Although you liberate
Pure and expensive fires
Fit to enamor Shebas,
Keep your desire apart.

Love only what you do,
And not what you have done.

Be proud, when you have set
The final spoke of flame
In that prismatic wheel,
And nothing's left this day
Except to see the sun
Shine on the false and the true,
And know that Africa
Will yield you more to do.

SNAPSHOTS

OF A

DAUGHTER-

IN-LAW

(1963)

AT MAJORITY
FOR C.

When you are old and beautiful,
And things most difficult are done,
There will be few who can recall
Your face that I see ravaged now
By youth and its oppressive work.

Your look will hold their wondering looks
Grave as Cordelia's at the last,
Neither with rancor at the past
Nor to upbraid the coming time.
For you will be at peace with time.

But now, a daily warfare takes
Its toll of tenderness in you,
And you must live like captains who
Wait out the hour before the charge—
Fearful, and yet impatient too.

Yet someday this will have an end,
All choices made or choice resigned,
And in your face the literal eye
Trace little of your history,
Nor ever piece the tale entire

Of villages that had to burn
And playgrounds of the will destroyed
Before you could be safe from time
And gather in your brow and air
The stillness of antiquity.

1954

FROM MORNING-GLORY TO PETERSBURG
(The World Book, *1928*)

"Organized knowledge in story and picture"
    confronts through dusty glass
    an eye grown dubious.
I can recall when knowledge still was pure,
    not contradictory, pleasurable
    as cutting out a paper doll.
You opened up a book and there it was:
    everything just as promised, from
    Kurdistan to Mormons, Gum
Arabic to Kumquat, neither more nor less.
    Facts could be kept separate
    by a convention; that was what
made childhood possible. Now knowledge finds me out;
    in all its risible untidiness
    it traces me to each address,
dragging in things I never thought about.
    I don't invite what facts can be
    held at arm's length; a family
of jeering irresponsibles always
    comes along gypsy-style
    and there you have them all
forever on your hands. It never pays.
    If I could still extrapolate
    the morning-glory on the gate
from Petersburg in history—but it's too late.

1954

RURAL REFLECTIONS

This is the grass your feet are planted on.
You paint it orange or you sing it green,
      But you have never found
A way to make the grass mean what you mean.

A cloud can be whatever you intend:
Ostrich or leaning tower or staring eye.
      But you have never found
A cloud sufficient to express the sky.

Get out there with your splendid expertise;
Raymond who cuts the meadow does no less.
      Inhuman nature says:
Inhuman patience is the true success.

Human impatience trips you as you run;
      Stand still and you must lie.
It is the grass that cuts the mower down;
It is the cloud that swallows up the sky.

1956

THE KNIGHT

A knight rides into the noon,
and his helmet points to the sun,
and a thousand splintered suns
are the gaiety of his mail.
The soles of his feet glitter
and his palms flash in reply,
and under his crackling banner
he rides like a ship in sail.

A knight rides into the noon,
and only his eye is living,
a lump of bitter jelly
set in a metal mask,
betraying rags and tatters
that cling to the flesh beneath
and wear his nerves to ribbons
under the radiant casque.

Who will unhorse this rider
and free him from between
the walls of iron, the emblems
crushing his chest with their weight?
Will they defeat him gently,
or leave him hurled on the green,
his rags and wounds still hidden
under the great breastplate?

1957

THE LOSER

A man thinks of the woman he once loved:
first, after her wedding, and then nearly a
decade later.

I.

I kissed you, bride and lost, and went
home from that bourgeois sacrament,
your cheek still tasting cold upon
my lips that gave you benison
with all the swagger that they knew—
as losers somehow learn to do.

Your wedding made my eyes ache; soon
the world would be worse off for one
more golden apple dropped to ground
without the least protesting sound,
and you would windfall lie, and we
forget your shimmer on the tree.

Beauty is always wasted: if
not Mignon's song sung to the deaf,
at all events to the unmoved.
A face like yours cannot be loved
long or seriously enough.
Almost, we seem to hold it off.

II.

Well, you are tougher than I thought.
Now when the wash with ice hangs taut
this morning of St. Valentine,
I see you strip the squeaking line,
your body weighed against the load,
and all my groans can do no good.

Because you still are beautiful,
though squared and stiffened by the pull
of what nine windy years have done.
You have three daughters, lost a son.
I see all your intelligence
flung into that unwearied stance.

My envy is of no avail.
I turn my head and wish him well
who chafed your beauty into use
and lives forever in a house
lit by the friction of your mind.
You stagger in against the wind.

1958

THE ABSENT-MINDED
ARE ALWAYS TO BLAME

What do you look for down there
in the cracks of the pavement? Or up there
between the pineapple and the acanthus leaf
in that uninspired ornament? Odysseus
wading half-naked out of the shrubbery
like a god, dead serious among those at play,
could hardly be more out of it. In school
we striped your back with chalk, you all oblivious,
your eyes harnessed by a transparent strand
reaching the other side of things, or down
like a wellchain to the center of earth.
Now with those same eyes you pull the
pavements up like old linoleum,
arches of triumph start to liquefy
minutes after you slowly turn away.

1958

EURYCLEA'S TALE

I have to weep when I see it, the grown boy fretting
for a father dawdling among the isles,
and the seascape hollowed out by that boy's edged gaze
to receive one speck, one only, for years and years withheld.

And that speck, that curious man, has kept from home
till home would seem the forbidden place, till blood
and the tears of an old woman must run down
to satisfy the genius of place. Even then, what
can they do together, father and son?
the driftwood stranger and the rooted boy
whose eyes will have nothing then to ask the sea.

But all the time and everywhere
lies in ambush for the distracted eyeball
light: light on the ship racked up in port,
the chimney-stones, the scar whiter than smoke,
than her flanks, her hair, that true but aging bride.

1958

SEPTEMBER 21

Wear the weight of equinoctial evening,
light like melons bruised on all the porches.
Feel the houses tenderly appraise you,
hold you in the watchfulness of mothers.

Once the nighttime was a milky river
washing past the swimmers in the sunset,
rinsing over sleepers of the morning.
Soon the night will be an eyeless quarry

where the shrunken daylight and its rebels,
loosened,   dive like stones in perfect silence,
names and voices drown without reflection.

Then the houses draw you. Then they have you.

1958

AFTER A SENTENCE
IN "MALTE LAURIDS BRIGGE"

The month's eye blurs.
The winter's lungs are cracked.
Along bloated gutters race,
shredded, your injured legions,
the waste of our remorseless search.
Your old, unuttered names are holes
worn in our skins
through which we feel from time to time
abrasive wind.

Those who are loved live poorly and in danger.
We who were loved will never
unlive that crippling fever.
A day returns, a certain weather
splatters the panes, and we
once more stare in the eye of our first failure.

1958

SNAPSHOTS OF A DAUGHTER-IN-LAW

1.

You, once a belle in Shreveport,
with henna-colored hair, skin like a peachbud,
still have your dresses copied from that time,
and play a Chopin prelude
called by Cortot: *"Delicious recollections*
float like perfume through the memory."

Your mind now, mouldering like wedding-cake,
heavy with useless experience, rich
with suspicion, rumor, fantasy,
crumbling to pieces under the knife-edge
of mere fact. In the prime of your life.

Nervy, glowering, your daughter
wipes the teaspoons, grows another way.

2.

Banging the coffee-pot into the sink
she hears the angels chiding, and looks out
past the raked gardens to the sloppy sky.
Only a week since They said: *Have no patience.*

The next time it was: *Be insatiable.*
Then: *Save yourself; others you cannot save.*
Sometimes she's let the tapstream scald her arm,
a match burn to her thumbnail,

or held her hand above the kettle's snout
right in the woolly steam. They are probably angels,
since nothing hurts her any more, except
each morning's grit blowing into her eyes.

3.

A thinking woman sleeps with monsters.
The beak that grips her, she becomes. And Nature,
that sprung-lidded, still commodious
steamer-trunk of *tempora* and *mores*
gets stuffed with it all: the mildewed orange-flowers,
the female pills, the terrible breasts
of Boadicea beneath flat foxes' heads and orchids.

Two handsome women, gripped in argument,
each proud, acute, subtle, I hear scream
across the cut glass and majolica
like Furies cornered from their prey:
The argument *ad feminam,* all the old knives
that have rusted in my back, I drive in yours,
ma semblable, ma soeur!

4.

Knowing themselves too well in one another:
their gifts no pure fruition, but a thorn,
the prick filed sharp against a hint of scorn . . .
Reading while waiting
for the iron to heat,
writing, *My Life had stood—a Loaded Gun—*
in that Amherst pantry while the jellies boil and scum,
or, more often,
iron-eyed and beaked and purposed as a bird,
dusting everything on the whatnot every day of life.

5.

Dulce ridens, dulce loquens,
she shaves her legs until they gleam
like petrified mammoth-tusk.

6.

When to her lute Corinna sings
neither words nor music are her own;
only the long hair dipping
over her cheek, only the song
of silk against her knees
and these
adjusted in reflections of an eye.

Poised, trembling and unsatisfied, before
an unlocked door, that cage of cages,
tell us, you bird, you tragical machine—
is this *fertilisante douleur?* Pinned down
by love, for you the only natural action,
are you edged more keen
to prise the secrets of the vault? has Nature shown
her household books to you, daughter-in-law,
that her sons never saw?

7.

*"To have in this uncertain world some stay
which cannot be undermined, is
of the utmost consequence."*
                              Thus wrote
a woman, partly brave and partly good,
who fought with what she partly understood.
Few men about her would or could do more,
hence she was labelled harpy, shrew and whore.

8.

"You all die at fifteen," said Diderot,
and turn part legend, part convention.
Still, eyes inaccurately dream
behind closed windows blankening with steam.

Deliciously, all that we might have been,
all that we were—fire, tears,
wit, taste, martyred ambition—
stirs like the memory of refused adultery
the drained and flagging bosom of our middle years.

9.

Not that it is done well, but
that it is done at all? Yes, think
of the odds! or shrug them off forever.
This luxury of the precocious child,
Time's precious chronic invalid,—
would we, darlings, resign it if we could?
Our blight has been our sinecure:
mere talent was enough for us—
glitter in fragments and rough drafts.

Sigh no more, ladies.
                          Time is male
and in his cups drinks to the fair.
Bemused by gallantry, we hear
our mediocrities over-praised,
indolence read as abnegation,
slattern thought styled intuition,
every lapse forgiven, our crime
only to cast too bold a shadow
or smash the mould straight off.

For that, solitary confinement,
tear gas, attrition shelling.
Few applicants for that honor.

10.

                              Well,

she's long about her coming, who must be
more merciless to herself than history.
Her mind full to the wind, I see her plunge
breasted and glancing through the currents,
taking the light upon her
at least as beautiful as any boy
or helicopter,
                    poised, still coming,
her fine blades making the air wince
but her cargo
no promise then:
delivered
palpable
ours.

1958–1960

PASSING ON

The landlord's hammer in the yard
patches a porch where your shirts swing
brashly against May's creamy blue.
This year the forsythia ran wild,
chrome splashed on the spring evenings,
every bush a pile of sulphur.
Now, ragged, they bend
under the late wind's onslaught, tousled
as my head beneath the clotheslines.

Soon we'll be off. I'll pack us into parcels,
stuff us in barrels, shroud us in newspapers,
pausing to marvel at old bargain sales:
Oh, all the chances we never seized!
Emptiness round the stoop of the house
minces, catwise, waiting for an in.

1959

THE RAVEN

If, antique hateful bird,
flapping through dawngagged streets
of metal shopfronts grated down
on pedestrian nerve-ends,

if, as on old film,
my features blurred and grained like cereal,
you find me walking up and down
waiting for my first dream,

don't try to sully my head
with vengeful squirtings. Fly on,
ratfooted cautionary of my dark,
till we meet further along.

You are no dream, old genius.
I smell you, get my teeth on edge,
stand in my sweat—in mercury—
even as you prime your feathers and set sail.

1959

MERELY TO KNOW

I.

Wedged in by earthworks
thrown up by snouters before me,
I kick and snuffle, breathing in
cobwebs of beetle-cuirass:
vainglory of polished green,
infallible pincer, resonant nerve,
a thickening on the air now,
confusion to my lungs, no more.
My predecessors blind me—
their zeal exhausted among roots and tunnels,
they gasped and looked up once or twice
into the beechtree's nightblack glitter.

II.

Let me take you by the hair
and drag you backward to the light,
there spongelike press my gaze
patiently upon your eyes,
hold like a photographic plate
against you my enormous question.
What if you cringe, what if you weep?
Suffer this and you need suffer
nothing more. I'll give you back
yourself at last to the last part.
I take nothing, only look.
Change nothing. Have no need to change.
Merely to know and let you go.

1959

III.

Spirit like water
molded by unseen stone
and sandbar, pleats and funnels
according to its own
submerged necessity—
to the indolent eye
pure willfulness, to the stray
pine-needle boiling
in that cascade-bent pool
a random fury: Law,
if that's what's wanted, lies
asking to be read
in the dried brock-bed.

1961

ANTINOÜS: THE DIARIES

Autumn torture. The old signs
smeared on the pavement, sopping leaves
rubbed into the landscape as unguent on a bruise,
brought indoors, even, as they bring flowers, enormous,
with the colors of the body's secret parts.
All this. And then, evenings, needing to be out,
walking fast, fighting the fire
that must die, light that sets my teeth on edge with joy,
till on the black embankment
I'm a cart stopped in the ruts of time.

Then at some house the rumor of truth and beauty
saturates a room like lilac-water
in the stream of a bath, fires snap, heads are high,
gold hair at napes of necks, gold in glasses,
gold in the throat, poetry of furs and manners.
Why do I shiver then? Haven't I seen,
over and over, before the end of an evening,
the three opened coffins carried in and left in a corner?
Haven't I watched as somebody cracked his shin
on one of them, winced and hopped and limped
laughing to lay his hand on a beautiful arm
striated with hairs of gold, like an almond-shell?

The old, needless story. For if I'm here
it is by choice and when at last
I smell my own rising nausea, feel the air
tighten around my stomach like a surgical bandage,
I can't pretend surprise. What is it I so miscarry?
If what I spew on the tiles at last,
helpless, disgraced, alone,
is in part what I've swallowed from glasses, eyes,
motions of hands, opening and closing mouths,

Isn't it also dead gobbets of myself,
abortive, murdered, or never willed?

1959

JUVENILIA

Your Ibsen volumes, violet-spined,
each flaking its gold arabesque!
Again I sit, under duress, hands washed,
at your inkstained oaken desk,
by the goose-neck lamp in the tropic of your books,
stabbing the blotting-pad, doodling loop upon loop,
peering one-eyed in the dusty reflecting mirror
of your student microscope,
craning my neck to spell above me

A DOLLS HOUSE   LITTLE EYOLF
        WHEN WE DEAD AWAKEN

Unspeakable fairy tales ebb like blood through my head
as I dip the pen and for aunts, for admiring friends,
for you above all to read,
copy my praised and sedulous lines.

Behind the two of us, thirsty spines
quiver in semi-shadow, huge leaves uncurl and thicken.

1960

DOUBLE MONOLOGUE

To live illusionless, in the abandoned mine-
    shaft of doubt, and still
mime illusions for others? A puzzle
    for the maker who has thought
once too often too coldly.

Since I was more than a child
    trying on a thousand faces
I have wanted one thing: to know
    simply as I know my name
at any given moment, where I stand.

How much expense of time and skill
    which might have set itself
to angelic fabrications! All merely
    to chart one needle in the haymow?
Find yourself and you find the world?

Solemn presumption! Mighty Object
    no one but itself has missed,
what's lost, if you stay lost? Someone
    ignorantly loves you—will that serve?
Shrug that off, and presto!—

the needle drowns in the haydust.
    Think of the whole haystack—
a composition so fortuitous
    it only looks monumental.
There's always a straw twitching somewhere.

Wait out the long chance, and
    your needle too could get nudged up
to the apex of that bristling calm.

Rusted, possibly. You might not want
to swear it was the Object, after all.

Time wears us old utopians.
    I now no longer think
"truth" is the most beautiful of words.
    Today, when I see "truthful"
written somewhere, it flares

like a white orchid in wet woods,
    rare and grief-delighting, up from the page.
Sometimes, unwittingly even,
    we have been truthful.
In a random universe, what more

exact and starry consolation?
    Don't think I think
facts serve better than ignorant love.
    Both serve, and still
our need mocks our gear.

1960

A WOMAN MOURNED
BY DAUGHTERS

Now, not a tear begun,
we sit here in your kitchen,
spent, you see, already.
You are swollen till you strain
this house and the whole sky.
You, whom we so often
succeeded in ignoring!
You are puffed up in death
like a corpse pulled from the sea;
we groan beneath your weight.
And yet you were a leaf,
a straw blown on the bed,
you had long since become
crisp as a dead insect.
What is it, if not you,
that settles on us now
like satin you pulled down
over our bridal heads?
What rises in our throats
like food you prodded in?
Nothing could be enough.
You breathe upon us now
through solid assertions
of yourself: teaspoons, goblets,
seas of carpet, a forest
of old plants to be watered,
an old man in an adjoining
room to be touched and fed.

And all this universe
dares us to lay a finger
anywhere, save exactly
as you would wish it done.

1960

READINGS OF HISTORY

He delighted in relating the fact that he had been born
near Girgenti in a place called Chaos during a raging
cholera epidemic.
                    —Domenico Vittorini, *The Drama of Luigi Pirandello*

I. *The Evil Eye*

Last night we sat with the stereopticon,
laughing at genre views of 1906,
till suddenly, gazing straight into
that fringed and tasselled parlor, where the vestal
spurns an unlikely suitor
with hairy-crested plants to right and left,
my heart sank. It was terrible.
I smelled the mildew in those swags of plush,
dust on the eyepiece bloomed to freaks of mold.
I knew beyond all doubt how dead that couple was.

Today, a fresh clean morning.
Your camera stabs me unawares,
right in my mortal part.
A womb of celluloid already
contains my dotage and my total absence.

II. *The Confrontation*

Luigi Pirandello
looked like an old historian
(oval head, tufted white beard,
not least the hunger
for reconciliation in his eye).
For fourteen years, facing
his criminal reflection
in his wife's Grand Guignol mind,
he built over and over

that hall of mirrors
in which to be appears
to be perceived.

The present holds you like a raving wife,
clever as the mad are clever,
digging up your secret truths
from her disabled genius.
She knows what you hope
and dare not hope:
remembers
what you're sick
of forgetting.
What are you now
but what you know together, you and she?

She will not let you think.
It is important
to make connections. Everything
happens very fast in the minds
of the insane. Even you
aren't up to that, yet.
Go out, walk,
think of selves long past.

III. *Memorabilia*

I recall
Civil War letters of a great-grand-uncle,
fifteen at Chancellorsville,
                    no raconteur,
no speller, either; nor to put it squarely,
much of a mind;
                    the most we gather
is that he did write home:
                    I am well,

how are my sisters, hope you are the same.
Did Spartan battle-echoes rack his head?
Dying, he turned into his father's memory.

History's queerly strong perfumes
rise from the crook of this day's elbow:
Seduction fantasies of the public mind,
or Dilthey's dream from which he roused to see
the cosmos glaring through his windowpane?
Prisoners of what we think occurred,
or dreamers dreaming toward a final word?

What, in fact, happened in these woods
on some obliterated afternoon?

IV. *Consanguinity*

Can history show us nothing
but pieces of ourselves, detached,
set to a kind of poetry,
a kind of music, even?
Seated today on Grandmamma's
plush sofa with the grapes
bursting so ripely from the curved mahogany,
we read the great Victorians
weeping, almost, as if
some family breach were healed.
Those angry giantesses and giants,
lately our kith and kin!
We stare into their faces, hear
at last what they were saying
(or some version not bruited
by filial irritation).

The cat-tails wither in the reading-room.
Tobacco-colored dust

drifts on the newest magazines.
I loaf here leafing ancient copies
of LIFE from World War II.
We look so poor and honest there:
girls with long hair badly combed
and unbecoming dresses—
where are you now?
                              You sail
to shop in Europe, ignorantly freed
for you, an age ago.
Your nylon luggage matches
                                        eyelids
expertly azured.
I, too, have lived in history.

V. *The Mirror*

Is it in hopes
to find or lose myself
that I
fill up my table now
with Michelet and Motley?
To "know how it was"
or to forget how it is—
what else?
Split at the root, neither Gentile nor Jew,
Yankee nor Rebel, born
in the face of two ancient cults,
I'm a good reader of histories.
And you,
Morris Cohen, dear to me as a brother,
when you sit at night
tracing your way through your volumes
of Josephus, or any
of the old Judaic chronicles,
do you find yourself there, a simpler,

more eloquent Jew?
                    or do you read
to shut out the tick-tock of self,
the questions and their routine answers?

VI. *The Covenant*

The present breaks our hearts. We lie and freeze,
our fingers icy as a bunch of keys.
Nothing will thaw these bones except
memory like an ancient blanket wrapped
about us when we sleep at home again,
smelling of picnics, closets, sicknesses,
old nightmare,
                    and insomnia's spreading stain.

Or say I sit with what I halfway know
as with a dying man who heaves the true
version at last, now that it hardly matters,
or gropes a hand to where the letters
sewn in the mattress can be plucked and read.
Here's water.   Sleep.   No more is asked of you.
I take your life into my living head.

1960

TO THE AIRPORT

Death's taxi crackles through the mist. The cheeks
of diamond battlements flush high and cold.
Alarm clocks strike a million sparks of will.
Weeping: all night we've wept and watched the hours
that never will be ours again: Now
weeping, we roll through unforgettable
Zion, that rears its golden head from sleep
to act, and does not need us as we weep.

You dreamed us, City, and you let us be.
Grandiloquence, improvidence, ordure, light,
hours that seemed years, and ours—and over all
the endless wing of possibility,
that mackerel heaven of yours, fretted with all
our wits could leap for, envy batten on.
Our flights take off from you into the sea;
nothing you need wastes, though we think we do.

You are Canaan now and we are lifted high
to see all we were promised, never knew.

1960

THE AFTERWAKE

Nursing your nerves
to rest, I've roused my own; well,
now for a few bad hours!
Sleep sees you behind closed doors.
Alone, I slump in his front parlor.
You're safe inside. Good. But I'm
like a midwife who at dawn
has all in order: bloodstains
washed up, teapot on the stove,
and starts her five miles home
walking, the birthyell still
exploding in her head.

Yes, I'm with her now: here's
the streaked, livid road
edged with shut houses
breathing night out and in.
Legs tight with fatigue,
we move under morning's coal-blue star,
colossal as this load
of unexpired purpose, which drains
slowly, till scissors of cockcrow snip the air.

1961

ARTIFICIAL INTELLIGENCE
TO GPS.

Over the chessboard now,
Your Artificiality concludes
a final check; rests; broods—
      no—sorts and stacks a file of memories,
while I
concede the victory, bow,
and slouch among my free associations.

You never had a mother,
let's say? no digital Gertrude
whom you'd as lief have seen
Kingless? So your White Queen
was just an "operator."
(My Red had incandescence,
ire, aura, flare,
and trapped me several moments in her stare.)

I'm sulking, clearly, in the great tradition
of human waste. Why not
dump the whole reeking snarl
and let you solve me once for all?
(*Parameter:* a black-faced Luddite
itching for ecstasies of sabotage.)

Still, when
they make you write your poems, later on,
who'd envy you, force-fed
on all those variorum
editions of our primitive endeavors,
those frozen pemmican language-rations
they'll cram you with? denied
our luxury of nausea, you
forget nothing, have no dreams.

1961

A MARRIAGE IN THE 'SIXTIES

As solid-seeming as antiquity,
you frown above
the *New York Sunday Times*
where Castro, like a walk-on out of *Carmen,*
mutters into a bearded henchman's ear.

They say the second's getting shorter—
I knew it in my bones—
and pieces of the universe are missing.
I feel the gears of this late afternoon
slip, cog by cog, even as I read.
"I'm old," we both complain,
half-laughing, oftener now.

Time serves you well. That face—
part Roman emperor, part Raimu—
nothing this side of Absence can undo.
Bliss, revulsion, your rare angers can
only carry through what's well begun.

When
I read your letters long ago
in that half-defunct
hotel in Magdalen Street
every word primed my nerves.
A geographical misery
composed of oceans, fogbound planes
and misdelivered cablegrams
lay round me, a Nova Zembla
only your live breath could unfreeze.
Today we stalk
in the raging desert of our thought
whose single drop of mercy is

each knows the other there.
Two strangers, thrust for life upon a rock,
may have at last the perfect hour of talk
that language aches for; still—
two minds, two messages.

Your brows knit into flourishes. Some piece
of mere time has you tangled there.
Some mote of history has flown into your eye.
Will nothing ever be the same,
even our quarrels take a different key,
our dreams exhume new metaphors?
The world breathes underneath our bed.
Don't look. We're at each other's mercy too.

Dear fellow-particle, electric dust
I'm blown with—ancestor
to what euphoric cluster—
see how particularity dissolves
in all that hints of chaos. Let one finger
hover toward you from There
and see this furious grain
suspend its dance to hang
beside you like your twin.

1961

FIRST THINGS

I can't name love now
without naming its object—
this the final measure
of those flintspark years
when one believed
one's flash innate.
Today I swear
only in the sun's eye
do I take fire.

1961

ATTENTION

The ice age is here.
I sit burning cigarettes,
burning my brain.
A micro-Tibet,
deadly, frivolous, complete,
blinds the four panes.
Veils of dumb air
unwind like bandages
from my lips
half-parted, steady as the mouths
of antique statues.

1961

END OF AN ERA

This morning, flakes of sun
peel down to the last snowholds,
the barbed-wire leavings of a war
lost, won, in these dead-end alleys.
Stale as a written-out journalist,
I sort my gear.—Nothing is happening.—City,
dumb as a pack of thumbed cards, you
once had snap and glare
and secret life; now, trembling
under my five grey senses' weight,
you flatten
onto the table.

Baudelaire, I think of you . . . Nothing changes,
rude and self-absorbed the current
dashes past, reflecting nothing, poetry
extends its unsought amnesty,
the roots of the great grove
atrophy underground.
Some voices, though, shake in the air like heat.

The neighborhood is changing,
even the neighbors are grown, methinks, peculiar.
I walk into my house and see
tourists fingering this and that.
My mirrors, my bric-à-brac
don't suit their style.

Those old friends, though,
alive and dead,
for whom things don't come easy—
Certain forests are sawdust,
from now on have to be described?
Nothing changes.   The bones of the mammoths
are still in the earth.

1961

RUSTICATION

In a gigantic *pot de chambre,* scrolled
with roses, purchased dearly at auction,
goldenrod and asters spill
toward the inevitable sunset.
The houseguests trail from swimming
under huge towels.
Marianne dangles barefoot in the hammock
reading about Martin Luther King.
Vivaldi rattles on the phonograph,
flutes ricocheting off the birchtrees.
Flies buzz and are gaily murdered.

Still out of it, and guilty,
I glue the distance-glasses to my eyes
ostrich-like, hoping
you'll think me in that clearing half a mile away.
Offstage I hear
the old time-killers dressing, banging doors,
your voice, a timbre or two too rich for love,
cheering them on.
A kestrel sails into my field of vision,
clear as a rising star.

Why should I need to quarrel
with another's consolations?
Why, in your mortal skin,
vigorously smashing ice and smoking,
a graying pigtail down your back,
should you seem infamous to me?

1961

APOLOGY

I've said: I wouldn't ever
keep a cat, a dog,
a bird—
chiefly because
I'd rather love my equals.
Today, turning
in the fog of my mind,
I knew, the thing I really
couldn't stand in the house
is a woman
with a mindful of fog
and bloodletting claws
and the nerves of a bird
and the nightmares of a dog.

1961

SISTERS

Can I easily say,
I know you of course now,
no longer the fellow-victim,
reader of my diaries, heir
to my outgrown dresses,
ear for my poems and invectives?
Do I know you better
than that blue-eyed stranger
self-absorbed as myself
raptly knitting or sleeping
through a thirdclass winter journey?
Face to face all night
her dreams and whimpers
tangled with mine,
sleeping but not asleep
behind the engine drilling
into dark Germany,
her eyes, mouth, head
reconstructed by dawn
as we nodded farewell.
Her I should recognize
years later, anywhere.

1961

IN THE NORTH

Mulish, unregenerate,
   not "as all men are"
   but more than most

you sit up there in the sunset;
   there are only three
   hours of dark

in your night. You are
   alone as an old king
   with his white-gold beard

when in summer the ships
   sail out, the heroes
   singing, push off

for other lands. Only
   in winter when
   trapped in the ice

your kingdom flashes
   under the northern lights
   and the bees dream

in their hives, the young
   men like the bees
   hang near you

for lack of another,
    remembering too, with some
    remorseful tenderness

you are their king.

1962

THE CLASSMATE

One year, you gave us
all names, hudibrastic
titles, skywrote
our gaudy histories.
We were all sparks
struck in your head,
we mocked but listened.
You filled a whole
zoological notebook
with sly generations
of should-have-beens,
were disgraced, not distressed.
Our howls died away.

Your poetry was in
paper-dart ballads
sailing beyond our noses,
in blackboard lyrics
scrawled in our own patois,
spirals of chalkdust,
inkblot manifestos
who could read today?
You less than any.
Because later you turned
to admiration of the classics
and a sedulous ear.

Still if I hear
the slash of feet
through gutters full of oakleaves
and see the boys
still unprized, unprizing,

dancing along, tossing
books and dusty leaves
into the sun,
they chant, it would seem,
your momentary quatrains,
nose-thumbing, free-lancing
poet of the schoolyard—
prize-giver and taker
now, a pillar
swaddled in laurels—
lost classmate, look!
your glory was here.

1962

PEELING ONIONS

Only to have a grief
equal to all these tears!

There's not a sob in my chest.
Dry-hearted as Peer Gynt
I pare away, no hero,
merely a cook.

Crying was labor, once
when I'd good cause.
Walking, I felt my eyes like wounds
raw in my head,
so postal-clerks, I thought, must stare.
A dog's look, a cat's, burnt to my brain—
yet all that stayed
stuffed in my lungs like smog.

These old tears in the chopping-bowl.

1961

GHOST OF A CHANCE

You see a man
trying to think.

You want to say
to everything:
Keep off! Give him room!
But you only watch,
terrified
the old consolations
will get him at last
like a fish
half-dead from flopping
and almost crawling
across the shingle,
almost breathing
the raw, agonizing
air
till a wave
pulls it back blind into the triumphant
sea.

1962

THE WELL

Down this old well
what leaves have fallen,
what cores of eaten apples,
what scraps of paper!
An old trash barrel.
November, no one comes.

But I come, trying
to breathe that word
into the well's ear
which could make the leaves fly up
like a green jet
to clothe the naked tree,
the whole fruit leap to the bough,
the scraps like fleets of letters
sail up into my hands.

Leiden, 1961

NOVELLA

Two people in a room, speaking harshly.
One gets up, goes out to walk.
(That is the man.)
The other goes into the next room
and washes the dishes, cracking one.
(That is the woman.)
It gets dark outside.
The children quarrel in the attic.
She has no blood left in her heart.
The man comes back to a dark house.
The only light is in the attic.
He has forgotten his key.
He rings at his own door
and hears sobbing on the stairs.
The lights go on in the house.
The door closes behind him.
Outside, separate as minds,
the stars too come alight.

1962

FACE

I could look at you a long time,
man of red and blue;
your eye glows mockingly
from the rainbow-colored flesh
Karel Appel clothed you in.
You are a fish,
drawn up dripping hugely
from the sea of paint,
laid on the canvas
to glower and flash
out of the blackness
that is your true element

1962

PROSPECTIVE
IMMIGRANTS
PLEASE NOTE

Either you will
go through this door
or you will not go through.

If you go through
there is always the risk
of remembering your name.

Things look at you doubly
and you must look back
and let them happen.

If you do not go through
it is possible
to live worthily

to maintain your attitudes
to hold your position
to die bravely

but much will blind you,
much will evade you,
at what cost who knows?

The door itself
makes no promises.
It is only a door.

1962

LIKENESS

A good man
   is an odd thing:
   hard to find
as the song says,

he is anarchic
   as a mountain freshet
   and unprotected
by the protectors.

1962

THE LAG

With you it is still the middle of the night.
Nothing I know will make you know
what birds cried me awake
or how the wet light leaked
into my sky.
Day came as no clear victory,
it's raining still, but light
washes the menace from obscure forms
and in the shaving mirror there's
a face I recognize.
With you it is still the middle of the night.

You hug yourself, tightened as in a berth
suspended over the Grand Banks
where time is already American
and hanging fire.
I'm older now than you.
I feel your black dreams struggling at a porthole
stuffed full of night. I feel you choking
in that thick place. My words
reach you as through a telephone
where some submarine echo of my voice
blurts knowledge you can't use.

1962

ALWAYS THE SAME

Slowly, Prometheus
bleeds to life
in his huge loneliness.

You, for whom
his bowels are exposed,
go about your affairs

dying a little every day
from the inside out
almost imperceptibly

till the late decades when
women go hysterical
and men are dumbly frightened

and far away, like the sea
Prometheus sings on
"like a battle-song after a battle."

1962

PEACE

Lashes of white light
binding another hailcloud—
the whole onset all over
bursting against our faces,
sputtering like dead holly
fired in a grate:
And the birds go mad
potted by grapeshot
while the sun shines
in one quarter of heaven
and the rainbow
breaks out its enormous flag—
oily, unnegotiable—
over the sack-draped backs
of the cattle in their kingdom.

1961

THE ROOFWALKER
FOR DENISE LEVERTOV.

Over the half-finished houses
night comes. The builders
stand on the roof. It is
quiet after the hammers,
the pulleys hang slack.
Giants, the roofwalkers,
on a listing deck, the wave
of darkness about to break
on their heads. The sky
is a torn sail where figures
pass magnified, shadows
on a burning deck.

I feel like them up there:
exposed, larger than life,
and due to break my neck.

Was it worth while to lay—
with infinite exertion—
a roof I can't live under?
—All those blueprints,
closings of gaps,
measurings, calculations?
A life I didn't choose
chose me: even
my tools are the wrong ones
for what I have to do.
I'm naked, ignorant,
a naked man fleeing
across the roofs
who could with a shade of difference
be sitting in the lamplight

against the cream wallpaper
reading—not with indifference—
about a naked man
fleeing across the roofs.

1961

POEMS

(1 9 5 5 – 1 9 5 7)

AT THE JEWISH NEW YEAR

For more than five thousand years
This calm September day
With yellow in the leaf
Has lain in the kernel of Time
While the world outside the walls
Has had its turbulent say
And history like a long
Snake has crawled on its way
And is crawling onward still.
And we have little to tell
On this or any feast
Except of the terrible past.
Five thousand years are cast
Down before the wondering child
Who must expiate them all.

Some of us have replied
In the bitterness of youth
Or the qualms of middle-age:
"If Time is unsatisfied,
And all our fathers have suffered
Can never be enough,
Why, then, we choose to forget.
Let our forgetting begin
With those age-old arguments
In which their minds were wound
Like musty phylacteries;
And we choose to forget as well
Those cherished histories
That made our old men fond,
And already are strange to us.

"Or let us, being today
Too rational to cry out,
Or trample underfoot
What after all preserves
A certain savor yet—
Though torn up by the roots—
Let us make our compromise
With the terror and the guilt
And view as curious relics
Once found in daily use
The mythology, the names
That, however Time has corrupted
Their ancient purity
Still burn like yellow flames,
But their fire is not for us."

And yet, however we choose
To deny or to remember,
Though on the calendars
We wake and suffer by,
This day is merely one
Of thirty in September—
In the kernel of the mind
The new year must renew
This day, as for our kind
Over five thousand years,
The task of being ourselves.
Whatever we strain to forget,
Our memory must be long.

May the taste of honey linger
Under the bitterest tongue.

1955

MOVING IN WINTER

Their life, collapsed like unplayed cards,
is carried piecemeal through the snow:
Headboard and footboard now, the bed
where she has lain desiring him
where overhead his sleep will build
its canopy to smother her once more;
their table, by four elbows worn
evening after evening while the wax runs down;
mirrors grey with reflecting them,
bureaus coffining from the cold
things that can shuffle in a drawer,
carpets rolled up around those echoes
which, shaken out, take wing and breed
new altercations, the old silences.

1957

NECESSITIES

OF LIFE

(1966)

I

POEMS 1962–1965

Changeray-je pas pour vous cette belle
contexture des choses? C'est la condition
de vostre creation, c'est une partie de
vous que la mort: vous vous fuyez vous-mesmes.

—Montaigne

NECESSITIES OF LIFE

Piece by piece I seem
to re-enter the world: I first began

a small, fixed dot, still see
that old myself, a dark-blue thumbtack

pushed into the scene,
a hard little head protruding

from the pointillist's buzz and bloom.
After a time the dot

begins to ooze. Certain heats
melt it.
        Now I was hurriedly

blurring into ranges
of burnt red, burning green,

whole biographies swam up and
swallowed me like Jonah.

Jonah! I was Wittgenstein,
Mary Wollstonecraft, the soul

of Louis Jouvet, dead
in a blown-up photograph.

Till, wolfed almost to shreds,
I learned to make myself

unappetizing. Scaly as a dry bulb
thrown into a cellar

I used myself, let nothing use me.
Like being on a private dole,

sometimes more like kneading bricks in Egypt.
What life was there, was mine,

now and again to lay
one hand on a warm brick

and touch the sun's ghost
with economical joy,

now and again to name
over the bare necessities.

So much for those days. Soon
practice may make me middling-perfect, I'll

dare inhabit the world
trenchant in motion as an eel, solid

as a cabbage-head. I have invitations:
a curl of mist steams upward

from a field, visible as my breath,
houses along a road stand waiting

like old women knitting, breathless
to tell their tales.

1962

IN THE WOODS

"Difficult ordinary happiness,"
no one nowadays believes in you.
I shift, full-length on the blanket,
to fix the sun precisely

behind the pine-tree's crest
so light spreads through the needles
alive as water just
where a snake has surfaced,

unreal as water in green crystal.
Bad news is always arriving.
"We're hiders, hiding from something bad,"
sings the little boy.

Writing these words in the woods,
I feel like a traitor to my friends,
even to my enemies.
The common lot's to die

a stranger's death and lie
rouged in the coffin, in a dress
chosen by the funeral director.
Perhaps that's why we never

see clocks on public buildings any more.
A fact no architect will mention.
We're hiders, hiding from something bad
most of the time.

Yet, and outrageously, something good
finds us, found me this morning
lying on a dusty blanket
among the burnt-out Indian pipes

and bursting-open lady's-slippers.
My soul, my helicopter, whirred
distantly, by habit, over
the old pond with the half-drowned boat

toward which it always veers
for consolation: ego's Arcady:
leaving the body stuck
like a leaf against a screen.—

Happiness! how many times
I've stranded on that word,
at the edge of that pond; seen
as if through tears, the dragon-fly—

only to find it all
going differently for once
this time: my soul wheeled back
and burst into my body.

Found! ready or not.
If I move now, the sun
naked between the trees
will melt me as I lie.

1963

THE CORPSE-PLANT

How dare a sick man, or an obedient man, write poems?

　　　　　　　　　　　　　　　　—Whitman

A milk-glass bowl hanging by three chains
from the discolored ceiling
is beautiful tonight. On the floor, leaves, crayons,
innocent dust foregather.

Neither obedient nor sick, I turn my head,
feeling the weight of a thick gold ring
in either lobe. I see the corpse-plants
clustered in a hobnailed tumbler

at my elbow, white as death, I'd say,
if I'd ever seen death;
whiter than life
next to my summer-stained hand.

Is it in the sun that truth begins?
Lying under that battering light
the first few hours of summer
I felt scraped clean, washed down

to ignorance. The gold in my ears,
souvenir of a shrewd old city,
might have been wearing thin as wires
found in the bones of a woman's head

miraculously kept in its essentials
in some hot cradle-tomb of time.
I felt my body slipping through
the fingers of its mind.

Later, I slid on wet rocks,
threw my shoes across a brook,
waded on algae-furred stones
to join them. That day I found

the corpse-plants, growing like
shadows on a negative
in the chill of fern and lichen-rust.
That day for the first time

I gave them their deathly names—
or did they name themselves?—
not "Indian pipes" as once
we children knew them.

Tonight, I think of winter,
winters of mind, of flesh,
sickness of the rot-smell of leaves
turned silt-black, heavy as tarpaulin,

obedience of the elevator cage
lowering itself, crank by crank
into the mine-pit,
forced labor forcibly renewed—

but the horror is dimmed:
like the negative of one
intolerable photograph
it barely sorts itself out

under the radiance of the milk-glass shade.
Only death's insect whiteness
crooks its neck in a tumbler
where I placed its sign by choice.

1963

THE TREES

The trees inside are moving out into the forest,
the forest that was empty all these days
where no bird could sit
no insect hide
no sun bury its feet in shadow
the forest that was empty all these nights
will be full of trees by morning.

All night the roots work
to disengage themselves from the cracks
in the veranda floor.
The leaves strain toward the glass
small twigs stiff with exertion
long-cramped boughs shuffling under the roof
like newly discharged patients
half-dazed, moving
to the clinic doors.

I sit inside, doors open to the veranda
writing long letters
in which I scarcely mention the departure
of the forest from the house.
The night is fresh, the whole moon shines
in a sky still open
the smell of leaves and lichen
still reaches like a voice into the rooms.
My head is full of whispers
which tomorrow will be silent.

Listen. The glass is breaking.
The trees are stumbling forward
into the night. Winds rush to meet them.
The moon is broken like a mirror,
its pieces flash now in the crown
of the tallest oak.

1963

LIKE THIS TOGETHER

FOR A.H.C.

1.

Wind rocks the car.
We sit parked by the river,
silence between our teeth.
Birds scatter across islands
of broken ice. Another time
I'd have said "Canada geese,"
knowing you love them.
A year, ten years from now
I'll remember this—
this sitting like drugged birds
in a glass case—
not why, only that we
were here like this together.

2.

They're tearing down, tearing up
this city, block by block.
Rooms cut in half
hang like flayed carcasses,
their old roses in rags,
famous streets have forgotten
where they were going. Only
a fact could be so dreamlike.
They're tearing down the houses
we met and lived in,
soon our two bodies will be all
left standing from that era.

3.

We have, as they say,
certain things in common.
I mean: a view
from a bathroom window
over slate to stiff pigeons
huddled every morning; the way
water tastes from our tap,
which you marvel at, letting
it splash into the glass.
Because of you I notice
the taste of water,
a luxury I might
otherwise have missed.

4.

Our words misunderstand us.
Sometimes at night
you are my mother:
old detailed griefs
twitch at my dreams, and I
crawl against you, fighting
for shelter, making you
my cave. Sometimes
you're the wave of birth
that drowns me in my first
nightmare. I suck the air.
Miscarried knowledge twists us
like hot sheets thrown askew.

5.

Dead winter doesn't die,
it wears away, a piece of carrion
picked clean at last,
rained away or burnt dry.
Our desiring does this,
make no mistake, I'm speaking
of fact: through mere indifference
we could prevent it.
Only our fierce attention
gets hyacinths out of those
hard cerebral lumps,
unwraps the wet buds down
the whole length of a stem.

1963

BREAKFAST IN A
BOWLING ALLEY IN
UTICA, NEW YORK

Smudged eyeballs,
mouth stale as air,
I'm newly dead, a corpse

so fresh the grave unnerves me.
Nobody here but me
and Hermes behind the counter

defrosting sandwich steaks.
Paeans of *vox humana*
sob from the walls. THIS LAND

IS MY LAND. . . . It sounds
mummified. Has no sex,
no liquor license.

I chew meat and bread
thinking of wheatfields—
a gold-beige ceinture—

and cattle like ghosts
of the buffalo, running
across plains, nearing

the abbatoir. Houses
dream old-fashionedly
in backwoods townships

while the land glitters
with temporary life
stuck fast by choice:

trailers put out taproots
of sewage pipe, suckers
of TV aerial—

but in one of them,
perhaps, a man
alone with his girl

for the first time.

1963

OPEN-AIR MUSEUM

Ailanthus, goldenrod, scrapiron, what makes you flower?
What burns in the dump today?

Thick flames in a grey field, tended
by two men: one derelict ghost,
one clearly apter at nursing destruction,
two priests in a grey field, tending the flames
of stripped-off rockwool, split
mattresses, a caved-in chickenhouse,
mad Lou's last stack of paintings, each a perfect black lozenge

seen from a train, stopped
as by design, to bring us
face to face with the flag of our true country:
violet-yellow, black-violet,
its heart sucked by slow fire
O my America
this then was your desire?

but you cannot burn fast enough:
in the photograph the white
skirts of the Harlem bride
are lashed by blown scraps, tabloid sheets,
and her beauty a scrap of flickering light
licked by a greater darkness

This then was your desire!
those trucked-off bad dreams
outside the city limits
crawl back in search of you, eyes
missing, skins missing, intenser in decay
the carriage that wheeled the defective baby
rolls up on three wheels

and the baby is still inside,
you cannot burn fast enough
Blue sparks of the chicory flower
flash from embers of the dump
inside the rose-rust carcass of a slaughtered Chevrolet
crouches the young ailanthus

and the two guardians go raking the sacred field, raking
slowly, to what endless end
Cry of truth among so many lies
at your heart burns on
a languid fire

1964

TWO SONGS

1.

Sex, as they harshly call it,
I fell into this morning
at ten o'clock, a drizzling hour
of traffic and wet newspapers.
I thought of him who yesterday
clearly didn't
turn me to a hot field
ready for plowing,
and longing for that young man
piercéd me to the roots
bathing every vein, etc.
All day he appears to me
touchingly desirable,
a prize one could wreck one's peace for.
I'd call it love if love
didn't take so many years
but lust too is a jewel
a sweet flower and what
pure happiness to know
all our high-toned questions
breed in a lively animal.

2.

That "old last act"!
And yet sometimes
all seems post coitum triste
and I a mere bystander.
Somebody else is going off,
getting shot to the moon.
Or, a moon-race!
Split seconds after my opposite number
lands
I make it—
we lie fainting together
at a crater-edge
heavy as mercury in our moonsuits
till he speaks—
in a different language
yet one I've picked up
through cultural exchanges . . .
we murmur the first moonwords:
Spasibo. Thanks. O.K.

1964

THE PARTING

The ocean twanging away there
and the islands like scattered laundry—

You can feel so free, so free,
standing on the headland

where the wild rose never stands still,
the petals blown off

before they fall
and the chicory nodding

blue, blue, in the all-day wind.
Barbed wire, dead at your feet,

is a kind of dune-vine,
the only one without movement.

Every knot is a knife
where two strands tangle to rust.

1963

NIGHT-PIECES: FOR A CHILD

THE CRIB

You sleeping I bend to cover.
Your eyelids work. I see
your dream, cloudy as a negative,
swimming underneath.
You blurt a cry. Your eyes
spring open, still filmed in dream.
Wider, they fix me—
—death's head, sphinx, medusa?
You scream.
Tears lick my cheeks, my knees
droop at your fear.
Mother I no more am,
but woman, and nightmare.

HER WAKING

Tonight I jerk astart in a dark
hourless as Hiroshima,
almost hearing you breathe
in a cot three doors away.

You still breathe, yes—
and my dream with its gift of knives,
its murderous hider and seeker,
ebbs away, recoils

back into the egg of dreams,
the vanishing point of mind.
All gone.

But you and I—
swaddled in a dumb dark
old as sickheartedness,
modern as pure annihilation—

we drift in ignorance.
If I could hear you now
mutter some gentle animal sound!
If milk flowed from my breast again. . . .

1964

THE STRANGER

Fond credos, plaster ecstasies!
We arrange a prison-temple

for the weak-legged little god
who might stamp the world to bits

or pull the sky in like a muslin curtain.
We hang his shrine with bells,

aeolian harps, paper windmills,
line it with biscuits and swansdown.

His lack of culture we expected,
scarcely his disdain however—

that wild hauteur, as if
it were we who blundered.

Wildness we fret to avenge!
Eye that hasn't yet blinked

on the unblinking gold archways
of its trance—*that* we know

must be trained away:
that aloof, selective stare.

Otherness that affronts us
as cats and dogs do not—

once this was original sin
beaten away with staves of holy writ.

Old simplemindedness. But the primal fault
of the little god still baffles.

All other strangers are forgiven
their strangeness, but he—

how save the eggshell world from his
reaching hands, how shield

ourselves from the disintegrating
blaze of his wide pure eye?

1964

AFTER DARK

I.

You are falling asleep and I sit looking at you
old tree of life
old man whose death I wanted
I can't stir you up now.

Faintly a phonograph needle
whirs round in the last groove
eating my heart to dust.
That terrible record! how it played

down years, wherever I was
in foreign languages even
over and over, *I know you better
than you know yourself   I know*

*you better than you know
yourself   I know
you*   until, self-maimed,
I limped off, torn at the roots,

stopped singing a whole year,
got a new body, new breath,
got children, croaked for words,
forgot to listen

or read your *mene tekel* fading on the wall,
woke up one morning
and knew myself your daughter.
Blood is a sacred poison.

Now, unasked, you give ground.
We only want to stifle
what's stifling us already.
Alive now, root to crown, I'd give

—oh,—something—not to know
our struggles now are ended.
I seem to hold you, cupped
in my hands, and disappearing.

When your memory fails—
no more to scourge my inconsistencies—
the sashcords of the world fly loose.
A window crashes

suddenly down. I go to the woodbox
and take a stick of kindling
to prop the sash again.
I grow protective toward the world.

II.

Now let's away from prison—
Underground seizures!
I used to huddle in the grave
I'd dug for you and bite

my tongue for fear it would babble
—Darling—
I thought they'd find me there
someday, sitting upright, shrunken,

my hair like roots and in my lap
a mess of broken pottery—
wasted libation—
and you embalmed beside me.

No, let's away. Even now
there's a walk between doomed elms
(whose like we shall not see much longer)
and something—grass and water—

an old dream-photograph.
I'll sit with you there and tease you
for wisdom, if you like,
waiting till the blunt barge

bumps along the shore.
Poppies burn in the twilight
like smudge pots.
I think you hardly see me

but—this is the dream now—
your fears blow out,
off, over the water.
At the last, your hand feels steady.

1964

MOURNING PICTURE

The picture is by Edwin Romanzo Elmer, 1850–1923.

They have carried the mahogany chair and the cane rocker
out under the lilac bush,
and my father and mother darkly sit there, in black clothes.
Our clapboard house stands fast on its hill,
my doll lies in her wicker pram
gazing at western Massachusetts.
This was our world.
I could remake each shaft of grass
feeling its rasp on my fingers,
draw out the map of every lilac leaf
or the net of veins on my father's
grief-tranced hand.

Out of my head, half-bursting,
still filling, the dream condenses—
shadows, crystals, ceilings, meadows, globes of dew.
Under the dull green of the lilacs, out in the light
carving each spoke of the pram, the turned porch-pillars,
under high early-summer clouds,
I am Effie, visible and invisible,
remembering and remembered.

They will move from the house,
give the toys and pets away.
Mute and rigid with loss my mother
will ride the train to Baptist Corner,
the silk-spool will run bare.
I tell you, the thread that bound us lies
faint as a web in the dew.
Should I make you, world, again,
could I give back the leaf its skeleton, the air
its early-summer cloud, the house
its noonday presence, shadowless,
and leave *this* out? I am Effie, you were my dream.

1965

"I AM IN DANGER—SIR—"

"Half-cracked" to Higginson, living,
afterward famous in garbled versions,
your hoard of dazzling scraps a battlefield,
now your old snood

mothballed at Harvard
and you in your variorum monument
equivocal to the end—
who are you?

Gardening the day-lily,
wiping the wine-glass stems,
your thought pulsed on behind
a forehead battered paper-thin,

you, woman, masculine
in single-mindedness,
for whom the word was more
than a symptom—

a condition of being.
Till the air buzzing with spoiled language
sang in your ears
of Perjury

and in your half-cracked way you chose
silence for entertainment,
chose to have it out at last
on your own premises.

1964

HALFWAY

IN MEMORY: M.G.J.

In the field the air writhes, a heat-pocket.
Masses of birds revolve, blades
of a harvester.
The sky is getting milkily white,
a sac of light is ready to burst open.

Time of hailstones and rainbow.
My life flows North. At last I understand.
A young girl, thought sleeping, is certified dead.
A tray of expensive waxen fruit,
she lies arranged on the spare-room coverlid.

To sit by the fire is to become another woman,
red hair charring to grey,
green eyes grappling with the printed page,
voice flailing, flailing , the uncomprehending.
My days lie open, listening, grandmother.

1965

AUTUMN SEQUENCE

1 .

An old shoe, an old pot, an old skin,
and dreams of the subtly tyrannical.
Thirst in the morning; waking into the blue

drought of another October
to read the familiar message nailed
to some burning bush or maple.

Breakfast under the pines, late yellow-
jackets fumbling for manna on the rim
of the stone crock of marmalade,

and shed pine-needles drifting
in the half-empty cup.
Generosity is drying out,

it's an act of will to remember
May's sticky-mouthed buds
on the provoked magnolias.

2.

Still, a sweetness hardly earned
by virtue or craft, belonging
by no desperate right to me

(as the marmalade to the wasp
who risked all in a last euphoria
of hunger)

washes the horizon. A quiet
after weeping, salt still on the tongue
is like this, when the autumn planet

looks me straight in the eye
and straight into the mind
plunges its impersonal spear:

Fill and flow over, think
till you weep, then sleep
to drink again.

3.

Your flag is dried-blood, turkey-comb
flayed stiff in the wind,
half-mast on the day of victory,

anarchist prince of evening marshes!
Your eye blurs in a wet smoke,
the stubble freezes under your heel,

the cornsilk *Mädchen* all hags now,
their gold teeth drawn,
the milkweeds gutted and rifled,

but not by you, foundering hero!
The future reconnoiters in dirty boots
along the cranberry-dark horizon.

Stars swim like grease-flecks
in that sky, night pulls a long knife.
Your empire drops to its knees in the dark.

4.

Skin of wet leaves on asphalt.
Charcoal slabs pitted with gold.
The reason for cities comes clear.

There must be a place, there has come a time—
where so many nerves are fusing—
for a purely moral loneliness.

Behind bloodsoaked lights of the avenues,
in the crystal grit of flying snow,
in this water-drop bulging at the taphead,

forced by dynamos three hundred miles
from the wild duck's landing and the otter's dive,
for three seconds of quivering identity.

There must be a place. But the eyeball stiffens
as night tightens and my hero passes out
with a film of stale gossip coating his tongue.

1964

NOON

Light pulses through underground chambers.
I have to tell myself: my eyes are not blue.
Two dark holes
feed at the sky.

It swirls through them, raging
in azure spirals.
Nothing changes them:
two black tubes, draining off

a lake of iris.
Cleave open my skull:
the gouts of blue
leap from the black grotto.

1965

NOT LIKE THAT

It's so pure in the cemetery.
The children love to play up here.
It's a little town, a game of blocks,
a village packed in a box,
a pre-war German toy.
The turf is a bedroom carpet:
heal-all, strawberry flower
and hillocks of moss.
To come and sit here forever,
a cup of tea on one's lap
and one's eyes closed lightly, lightly,
perfectly still
in a nineteenth-century sleep!
it seems so normal to die.

Nobody sleeps here, children.
The little beds of white wrought iron
and the tall, kind, faceless nurse
are somewhere else, in a hospital
or the dreams of prisoners of war.
The drawers of this trunk are empty,
not even a snapshot
curls in a corner.

In Pullmans of childhood we lay
enthralled behind dark-green curtains,
and a little lamp burned blue
all night, for us. The day
was a dream too, even the oatmeal
under its silver lid, dream-cereal
spooned out in forests of spruce
skirting the green-black gorges,
thick woods of sleep, half prickle,

half lakes of fern.
To stay here forever
is not like that, nor even
simply to lie quite still,
the warm trickle of dream
staining the thick quiet.
The drawers of this trunk are empty.
They are all out of sleep up here.

1965

THE KNOT

In the heart of the queen anne's lace, a knot of blood.
For years I never saw it,

years of metallic vision,
spears glancing off a bright eyeball,

suns off a Swiss lake.
A foaming meadow; the Milky Way;

and there, all along, the tiny dark-red spider
sitting in the whiteness of the bridal web,

waiting to plunge his crimson knifepoint
into the white apparencies.

Little wonder the eye, healing, sees
for a long time through a mist of blood.

1965

ANY HUSBAND TO ANY WIFE

"Might I die last and show thee!"

I know: you are glycerine,
old quills, rose velvet,
tearstains in *Middlemarch*,
a style of getting into cabs, of eating fruit,
a drawer of stones, chains, seeds, shells, little mirrors:
Darling, you will outlive yourself, and me.

Sometimes the sea backs up against a lashed pier,
grinding and twisting,
a turmoil of wrecked stuff
alive and dead. And the pier stands groaning
as if the land depended on it.
We say it is the moon that draws these tides,
then glazes in aftercalm
the black, blurred face to something we can love.

1965

SIDE BY SIDE

Ho! in the dawn
how light we lie

stirring faintly as laundry
left all night on the lines.

You, a lemon-gold pyjama,
I, a trousseau-sheet, fine

linen worn paper-thin in places,
worked with the maiden monogram.

Lassitude drapes our folds.
We're slowly bleaching

with the days, the hours, and the years.
We are getting finer than ever,

time is wearing us to silk,
to sheer spiderweb.

The eye of the sun, rising, looks in
to ascertain how we are coming on.

1965

SPRING THUNDER

1.

Thunder is all it is, and yet
my street becomes a crack in the western hemisphere,
my house a fragile nest of grasses.

The radiotelescope flings its nets
at random; a child is crying,
not from hunger, not from pain,
more likely impotence. The generals are sweltering

in the room with a thousand eyes.
Red-hot lights flash off and on
inside air-conditioned skulls.

Underfoot, a land-mass
puffed-up with bad faith and fatigue
goes lumbering onward,

old raft in the swollen waters,
unreformed Huck and Jim
watching the tangled yellow shores
rush by.

2.

Whatever you are that weeps
over the blistered riverbeds
and the cracked skin of cities,
you are not on our side,

eye never seeking our eyes,
shedding its griefs like stars
over our hectic indifference,
whispered monologue

subverting space with its tears,
mourning the mournable,
nailing the pale-grey woolly flower
back to its ledge.

3.

The power of the dinosaur
is ours, to die
inflicting death,
trampling the nested grasses:

power of dead grass
to catch fire
power of ash
to whirl off the burnt heap
in the wind's own time.

4.

A soldier is here, an ancient figure,
generalized as a basalt mask.

Breathes like a rabbit, an Eskimo,
strips to an older and simpler thing.

No criminal, no hero; merely a shadow
cast by the conflagration

that here burns down or there leaps higher
but always in the shape of fire,

always the method of fire, casting
automatically, these shadows.

5.

Over him, over you, a great roof is rising,
a great wall: no temporary shelter.
Did you tell yourself these beams would melt,

these fiery blocs dissolve?
Did you choose to build this thing?
Have you stepped back to see what it is?

It is immense; it has porches, catacombs.
It is provisioned like the Pyramids, for eternity.
Its buttresses beat back the air with iron tendons.

It is the first flying cathedral,
eating its parishes by the light of the moon.
It is the refinery of pure abstraction,

a total logic, rising
obscurely between one man
and the old, affective clouds.

1965

MOTH HOUR

Space mildews at our touch.
The leaves of the poplar, slowly moving—
aren't they moth-white, there in the moonbeams?
A million insects die every twilight,
no one even finds their corpses.
Death, slowly moving among the bleached clouds,
knows us better than we know ourselves.

I am gliding backward away from those who knew me
as the moon grows thinner and finally shuts its lantern.
I can be replaced a thousand times,
a box containing death.
When you put out your hand to touch me
you are already reaching toward an empty space.

1965

FOCUS
FOR BERT DREYFUS.

Obscurity has its tale to tell.
Like the figure on the studio-bed in the corner,

out of range, smoking, watching and waiting.
Sun pours through the skylight onto the worktable

making of a jar of pencils, a typewriter keyboard
more than they were. Veridical light . . .

Earth budges. Now an empty coffee-cup,
a whetstone, a handkerchief, take on

their sacramental clarity, fixed by the wand
of light as the thinker thinks to fix them in the mind.

O secret in the core of the whetstone, in the five
pencils splayed out like fingers of a hand!

The mind's passion is all for singling out.
Obscurity has another tale to tell.

1965

FACE TO FACE

Never to be lonely like that—
the Early American figure on the beach
in black coat and knee-breeches
scanning the didactic storm in privacy,

never to hear the prairie wolves
in their lunar hilarity
circling one's little all, one's claim
to be Law and Prophets

for all that lawlessness,
never to whet the appetite
weeks early, for a face, a hand
longed-for and dreaded—

How people used to meet!
starved, intense, the old
Christmas gifts saved up till spring,
and the old plain words,

and each with his God-given secret,
spelled out through months of snow and silence,
burning under the bleached scalp; behind dry lips
a loaded gun.

1965

II

TRANSLATIONS FROM THE DUTCH

These translations are from a group commissioned by the Bollingen Foundation. For criticism and linguistic advice my thanks go to Judith Herzberg, Marjan DeWolff, and Leo Vroman; the final responsibility is of course my own.

MARTINUS NIJHOFF
THE SONG OF THE FOOLISH BEES

A smell of further honey
embittered nearer flowers,
a smell of further honey
sirened us from our meadow.

That smell and a soft humming
crystallized in the azure,
that smell and a soft humming,
a wordless repetition,

called upon us, the reckless,
to leave our usual gardens,
called upon us, the reckless,
to seek mysterious roses.

Far from our folk and kindred
joyous we went careering,
far from our folk and kindred
exhuberantly driven.

No one can by nature
break off the course of passion,
no one can by nature
endure death in his body.

Always more fiercely yielding,
more lucently transfigured,
always more fiercely yielding
to that elusive token,

we rose and staggered upward,
kidnapped, disembodied,
we rose and vanished upward,
dissolving into glitter.

It's snowing; we are dying,
homeward, downward whirled.
It's snowing; we are dying;
it snows among the hives.

HENDRIK DE VRIES
MY BROTHER

My brother, nobody knows
the end you suffered.
Often you lie beside me, dim, and I
grow confused, grope, and startle.

You walked along that path through the elms.
Birds cried late. Something wrong
was following us both. But you
wanted to go alone through the waste.

Last night we slept again together.
Your heart jerked next to me. I spoke your name
and asked where you were going.
Your answer came:
"The horror! . . . there's no telling . . .
See: the grass
lies dense again, the elms
press round."

HENDRIK DE VRIES
FEVER

Listen! It's never sung like that! Listen!
The wallpaper stirred,
and the hairs of the heavy-fringed eye.
What flew
through the rooms?

Tomorrow it will be
as if all night the whips hadn't lashed so.—

See, through the blinds,
the spirits in their cold ships!

Boughs graze the frame
of the window. Far off, a whistle
sounds, always clearly, along the fields.
The beasts on the walls
fade away. The light goes out.

GERRIT ACHTERBERG
EBEN HAËZER

(Hebrew for "Stone of Help"; a common old name
for farmhouses in Holland.)

Sabbath evening privacy at home.
Mist-footsteps, prowling past the shed.
At that hour, not another soul abroad;
the blue farmhouse a closed hermitage.

There we lived together, man and mouse.
Through cowstall windows an eternal fire
fell ridged from gold lamps on the threshing-floor,
stillness of linseed cakes and hay in house.

There my father celebrated mass:
serving the cows, priestlike at their heads.
Their tongues curled along his hands like fish.

A shadow, diagonal to the rafters.
Worship hung heavy from the loftbeams.
His arteries begin to calcify.

GERRIT ACHTERBERG
ACCOUNTABILITY

Old oblivion-book, that I lay open.
White eye-corner rounding the page.

Gold lace slips out under the evening,
Green animals creep backwards.

Lifelessness of the experimental station.
Added-up, subtracted sum.

Black night. Over the starlight skims
God's index finger, turning the page.

Death comes walking on all fours
past the room, a crystal egg,

with the lamp, the books, the bread,
where you are living and life-size.

GERRIT ACHTERBERG
STATUE

A body, blind with sleep,
stands up in my arms.
Its heaviness weighs on me.
Death-doll.
I'm an eternity too late.
And where's your heartbeat?

The thick night glues us together,
makes us compact with each other.
"For God's sake go on holding me—
my knees are broken,"
you mumble against my heart.

It's as if I held up the earth.
And slowly, moss is creeping
all over our two figures.

Leo Vroman
OUR FAMILY

My father, who since his death
no longer speaks audibly
lies sometimes, a great walrus
from nightfall to daybreak
his muzzle in my lap
in the street from his chin down.

The light of morning feeds
through his hide, thinned to parchment,
and his slackened features dwindle
to a line creeping off among the chairs;
if I rise to peer at him
he winces away to a dot

In the daytime there's nothing to see
but an emphatically vanished
absence where moments ago
the sun too was just shining.

Where my father has stood
it now just quivers,
rippling by handfuls through
my little daughter's light hair
while on the sunny grass
she slowly scampers forward.

Her little snoot is so open
you could easily spread it out
with a teaspoon or your finger
on a slice of fresh white bread
or, if need be,
you could mold it into a pudding.

Her little voice itches like a fleece;
it wriggles gaily into my ear
and can't get out when it laughs;
with plopping fishfins
it folds itself struggling up
into my head. Where it spends the night.

And here, this taller child
is Tineke, my wife.
She hums a nursery rhyme
to the hair on her third breast,
which whimpers, being a baby,
and a thirsty baby at that.

I have such a gentle family,
it kisses, goes on eight legs,
but it has no moustache:
my father has vanished,

and they too are all going to die:
too soft, if they turn into air,
to swing a weathercock;
if turned into water, too slight
to fill a gutter; if into light
to make one live cock crow.

CHR. J. VAN GEEL
HOMECOMING

The sea, a body of mysterious calls
is almost motionless.
I know a beach, a tree stands there
in which women are singing,
voluptuous, languid.

In harbors ships are steaming
full of honey from the sea. Drizzle hangs
like eyelashes over the landscape.

Behind the seadlike, breathing invisibly
in the mist, sleep the cows.
The hobble of a horse drags along the fence,
holding still where I stand with sweet words.

Listen, the sea calls,
claps her hands.
The ships running out in the wet
come like children—one drags
a sled into the garden.

CHR. J. VAN GEEL
SLEEPWALKING

(next to death.)

Sleep, horns of a snail

Out of the black and white bed, floors of red glaze,
mornings in the careful garden
on paths suitable rubbish slowly buried
and without urgency overgrown with grass
with ivy and sometimes a flower
just as we dream
to see unseen, to listen unattended.

The twigs of the moon
in indifferent white,
horns upright, wood with-
out leaf and seeking bees
sadness down to the ground.

Like silence always and from afar
lisps the water
never, by no one possessed.

Dead trees in green leaf.
What to do but among bushes,
what to see but underbrush.

On this sun time sharpens itself
to brilliance.

A stone of untouchable fire
on which time breaks its tooth.

Time caught no hour: loafing next to
a blaze.

In the darkened town the old groped
                    with their sticks.
The rays of the sun are tired,
the beetles rot in the wood,
only the sea. . . .
In the earth of the dead
earth covers leaf, leaf covers leaf.

Heartbeat of the wild creeper,
hammer between wing-lashes,
butterflies hammer at the sun.

Now you must get to the institution
with a mask on, your little feet
tarred, an iron crown on your head.

You awake there a python,
a boa constrictor,
after seven-and-twenty years,
after six-and-twenty years,
fair sleep, fair sleepers.

You strike the prince twice
a youth wasted with waiting
for your serpent eyes and
you unfold your scaly tail.

Now you must get to the institution
with a mask on, your little feet
tarred, an iron crown on your head.

Night blows away from the sun,
sky in fresh wind,
the sea kicks off its surf.

The moon scorches, a cloud of steam.
Driving water torn to shreds,
sunny twilight, fruitless field.

Tamed sea, muscular
to the temples, stoop where no coast
is, under the familiar blows,
stand where you cannot stand,
night is embraced on the sun.

A scared hind in a wood of one tree.

Whether the dead live, how they rest or
decay, leaves me cold, for cold for good and all
is death.

Poor is the frontier of life, to die blossoms
away over the graves.

Every existence competes in every
lost chance of life for death.

Of always fewer chances, one moved
and drove over her, naked standing by her child
death.

Residing in a thunderstorm,
sky hoists sun, night cuts light.
The wind's wings are at home.

Whistle now out of the nights
sparks of burnt paper.
Whisper fire in the days
dried by the sun, your desires
are lightened, curled to ash.

Flowers for hunger,

the darkest, the blue,
of ash, of grey granite,
black ice,
room without window,
abacus without beads,
room without a person,
the eaten past
gnaws,
the teeth out of the comb,
the funeral wreath emptily devoured,
a stone.

Whatever I may contrive—
and I contrive it—death's
private roads are the coldest night.

That I shall not be with her—
not with her—
that nothing shall glimmer
except danger.

Trees of ash, trees of ice,
the light frozen.
Summer and winter are
constructed of one emptiness.
The boughs of the wind are dead.

Must I dejected and contemplating death
now that above the sea a cloudless night
empties the sky, let treason and false laughter
prudently ring out until the morning?

the threshold of the horizon shifts—
and think with the thinkers of this earth:
"Life is thus"—then am I crazed
because my heart encloses what it held?

Morning has broken and the sea
is wide, I go back home to sleep.
Path, dune, trees and sheep
are rosy from the east, a rosy gull
flies up under the rash sky.
What's silent speaks aloud buried in sleep.

POEMS

(1962 – 1965)

TO JUDITH, TAKING LEAVE

FOR J.H.

Dull-headed, with dull fingers
I patch once more
the pale brown envelope
still showing under ink scratches
the letterhead of *Mind.*
A chorus of old postmarks
echoes across its face.
It looks so frail
to send so far
and I should tear it across
mindlessly
and find another.
But I'm tired, can't endure
a single new motion
or room or object,
so I cling to this too
as if your tallness moving
against the rainlight
in an Amsterdam flat
might be held awhile
by a handwritten label
or a battered envelope
from your desk.

Once somewhere else
I shan't talk of you
as a singular event
or a beautiful thing I saw
though both are true.
I shan't falsify you
through praising and describing
as I shall other

things I have loved
almost as much.
There in Amsterdam
you'll be living as I
have seen you live
and as I've never seen you.
And I can trust
no plane to bring you
my life out there
in turbid America—
my own life, lived against
facts I keep there.

It wasn't literacy—
the right to read *Mind*—
or suffrage—to vote
for the lesser of two
evils—that were
the great gains, I see now,
when I think of all those women
who suffered ridicule
for us.
But this little piece of ground,
Judith! that two women
in love to the nerves' limit
with two men—
shared out in pieces
to men, children, memories
so different and so draining—
should think it possible
now for the first time
perhaps, to love each other
neither as fellow-victims
nor as a temporary
shadow of something better.
Still shared-out as we are,

lovers, poets, warmers
of men and children
against our flesh, not knowing
from day to day
what we'll fling out on the water
or what pick up
there at the tide's lip,
often tired, as I'm tired now
from sheer distances of soul
we have in one day to cover—
still to get here
to this little spur or headland
and feel now free enough
to leave our weapons somewhere
else—such are the secret
outcomes of revolution!
that two women can meet
no longer as cramped sharers
of a bitter mutual secret
but as two eyes in one brow
receiving at one moment
the rainbow of the world.

1962

ROOTS
FOR M.L.

Evenings seem endless, now
dark tugs at our sky
harder and earlier
and milkweeds swell to bursting . . .
now in my transatlantic eye
you stand on your terrace
a scarf on your head and in your hands
dead stalks of golden-glow

and now it's for you,
not myself, I shiver
hearing glass doors rattle
at your back, the rustling cough
of a dry clematis vine
your love and toil trained up the walls
of a rented house.

All those roots, Margo!
Didn't you start each slip between your breasts,
each dry seed, carrying some
across frontiers, knotted
into your handkerchief,
haven't you seen your tears
glisten in narrow trenches
where rooted cuttings grope for life?

You, frailer than you look,
long back, long stride, blond hair
coiled up over straight shoulders—
I hear in your ear the wind
lashing in wet from the North Sea
slamming the dahlias flat.

All your work violated
every autumn, every turn of the wrist
guiding the trowel: mocked.
Sleet on brown fibers,
black wilt eating your harvest,
a clean sweep, and you the loser . . .

or is this after all
the liberation your hands fend off
and your eyes implore
when you dream of sudden death
or of beginning anew,
a girl of seventeen, the war just over,
and all the gardens
to dig again?

1963

THE PARTING: II

White morning flows into the mirror.
Her eye, still old with sleep,
meets itself like a sister.

How they slept last night,
the dream that caged them back to back,
was nothing new.

Last words, tears, most often
come wrapped as the everyday
familiar failure.

Now, pulling the comb slowly
through her loosened hair
she tries to find the parting;

it must come out after all:
hidden in all that tangle
there is a way.

1963

WHITE NIGHT

From the Yiddish of Kadia Molodowsky.

White night, my painful joy,
your light is brighter than the dawn.
A white ship is sailing from East Broadway
where I see no sail by day.

A quiet star hands me a ticket
open for all the seas,
I put on my time-worn jacket
and entrust myself to the night.

Where are you taking me, ship?
Who charted us on this course?
The hieroglyphs of the map escape me,
and the arrows of your compass.

I am the one who sees and does not see.
I go along on your deck of secrets,
squeeze shut my baggage on the wreath of sorrows
from all my plucked-out homes.

—Pack in all my blackened pots,
their split lids, the chipped crockeries,
pack in my chaos with its gold-encrusted buttons
since chaos will always be in fashion.

—Pack the letters stamped *Unknown at This Address*—
vanished addresses that sear my eyes,
postmarked with more than years and days;
sucked into my bones and marrow.

—Pack up my shadow that weighs more than my body,
that comes along with its endless exhortations.
Weekdays or holidays, time of flowers or withering,
my shadow is with me, muttering its troubles.

Find me a place of honey cakes and sweetness
where angels and children picnic together
(this is the dream I love best of all),
where the sacred wine fizzes in bottles.

Let me have one sip, here on East Broadway,
for the sake of those old Jews crying in the dark.
I cry my heretic's tears with them,
their sobbing is my sobbing.

I'm a difficult passenger, my ship
is packed with the heavy horns, the *shofars* of grief.
Tighten the sails of night as far as you can,
for the daylight cannot carry me.

Take me somewhere to a place of rest,
of goats in belled hats playing on trombones—
to the Almighty's fresh white sheets
where the hunter's shadow cannot fall.

Take me . . . Yes, take me . . . But you know best
where the sea calmly opens its blue road.
I'm wearier than your oldest tower;
somewhere I've left my heart aside.

1968

WINTER

Dead, dead, dead, dead.
A beast of the Middle Ages
stupefied in its den.
The hairs on its body—a woman's—
cold as hairs on a bulb or tuber.

Nothing so bleakly leaden, you tell me,
as the hyacinth's dull cone
before it bulks into blueness.
Ah, but I'd chosen to be
a woman, not a beast or a tuber!

No one knows where the storks went,
everyone knows they have disappeared.
Something—that woman—seems to have
migrated also; if she lives, she lives
sea-zones away, and the meaning grows colder.

1965

LEAFLETS

(1969)

For Rose Marie and Hayden Carruth

I

NIGHT WATCH

ORION

Far back when I went zig-zagging
through tamarack pastures
you were my genius, you
my cast-iron Viking, my helmed
lion-heart king in prison.
Years later now you're young

my fierce half-brother, staring
down from that simplified west
your breast open, your belt dragged down
by an oldfashioned thing, a sword
the last bravado you won't give over
though it weighs you down as you stride

and the stars in it are dim
and maybe have stopped burning.
But you burn, and I know it;
as I throw back my head to take you in
an old transfusion happens again:
divine astronomy is nothing to it.

Indoors I bruise and blunder,
break faith, leave ill enough
alone, a dead child born in the dark.
Night cracks up over the chimney,
pieces of time, frozen geodes
come showering down in the grate.

A man reaches behind my eyes
and finds them empty
a woman's head turns away
from my head in the mirror
children are dying my death
and eating crumbs of my life.

Pity is not your forte.
Calmly you ache up there
pinned aloft in your crow's nest,
my speechless pirate!
You take it all for granted
and when I look you back

it's with a starlike eye
shooting its cold and egotistical spear
where it can do least damage.
Breathe deep! No hurt, no pardon
out here in the cold with you
you with your back to the wall.

1965

HOLDING OUT

The hunters' shack will do,
abandoned, untended, unmended
in its cul-de-sac of alders.
Inside, who knows what
hovel-keeping essentials—
a grey saucepan, a broom, a clock
stopped at last autumn's last hour—
all or any, what matter.

The point is, it's a shelter,
a place more in- than outside.
From that we could begin.
And the wind is surely rising,
snow is in the alders.
Maybe the stovepipe is sound,
maybe the smoke will do us in
at first—no matter.

Late afternoons the ice
squeaks underfoot like mica,
and when the sun drops red and moon-
faced back of the gun-colored firs,
the best intentions are none too good.
Then we have to make a go of it
in the smoke with the dark outside
and our love in our boots at first—
no matter.

1965

FLESH AND BLOOD
FOR C.

A cracked walk in the garden,
white violets choking in the ivy,
then, O then . . .
Everyone else I've had to tell how it was,
only not you.

Nerve-white, the cloud came walking
over the crests of tallest trees.
Doors slammed. We
fell asleep, hot Sundays, in our slips,
two mad little goldfish

fluttering in a drying pond.
Nobody's seen the trouble I've seen
but you.
Our jokes are funnier for that
you'd say
and, Lord, it's true.

1965

IN THE EVENING

Three hours chain-smoking words
and you move on. We stand in the porch,
two archaic figures: a woman and a man.

The old masters, the old sources,
haven't a clue what we're about,
shivering here in the half-dark 'sixties.

Our minds hover in a famous impasse
and cling together. Your hand
grips mine like a railing on an icy night.

The wall of the house is bleeding. Firethorn!
The moon, cracked every which-way,
pushes steadily on.

1966

MISSING THE POINT

There it was, all along,
twisted up in that green vine-thread,
in the skeins of marble,
on the table behind them—those two!
white-faced and undeterred—
everything doubled: forks,
brown glass tumblers, echoing plates,
two crumbled portions of bread.

That was the point that was missed
when they left the room with its wavy light
and pale curtains blowing
and guessed the banquet was over, the picnic
under the leaves was over,
when haggling faces pushed in for a look
and the gingerbread village shrieked outside:
Who's in the wrong? Who's in the wrong?

1966

CITY

From the Dutch of Gerrit Achterberg.

Maybe you spoke to someone
and on that hour your face
printed itself for good.
Where is that man? I need
to find him before he dies
and see you drift across his retina.

You have played with children.
They will run up to me
whenever you
come home free in their dreams.

Houses, realized by you,
slumber in that web.

Streets suppose you
in other streets, and call:
Evening papers . . .
Strawberries . . .

The city has changed hands;
the plan you gave it, fallen through.

1962

DWINGELO

From the Dutch of Gerrit Achterberg.

In the never, still arriving, I find you
again: blue absence keeps knowledge alive,
makes of October an adjusted lens.
The days have almost no clouds left.

Cassiopeia, the Great Bear
let their signals burst by night
to rip into impossibility.
The Pleiades rage silently about.

To wait is the password; and to listen.
In Dwingelo you can hear it whisper,
the void in the radiotelescope.

There too the singing of your nerves is gathered,
becoming graphic on a sheet of paper
not unlike this one here.

1962

THE DEMON LOVER

Fatigue, regrets. The lights
go out in the parking lot
two by two. Snow blindness
settles over the suburb.
Desire. Desire. The nebula
opens in space, unseen,
your heart utters its great beats
in solitude. A new
era is coming in.
Gauche as we are, it seems
we have to play our part.

A plaid dress, silk scarf,
and eyes that go on stinging.
Woman, stand off. The air
glistens like silk.
She's gone. In her place stands
a schoolgirl, morning light,
the half-grown bones
of innocence. Is she
your daughter or your muse,
this tree of blondness
grown up in a field of thorns?

Something piercing and marred.
Take note. Look back. When quick
the whole northeast went black
and prisoners howled and children
ran through the night with candles,
who stood off motionless
side by side while the moon swam up
over the drowned houses?
Who neither touched nor spoke?

whose nape, whose finger-ends
nervelessly lied the hours away?

A voice presses at me.
If I give in it won't
be like the girl the bull rode,
all Rubens flesh and happy moans.
But to be wrestled like a boy
with tongue, hips, knees, nerves, brain . . .
with language?
He doesn't know. He's watching
breasts under a striped blouse,
his bull's head down.
The old wine pours again through my veins.

Goodnight, then. 'Night. Again
we turn our backs and weary
weary we let down.
Things take us hard, no question.
How do you make it, all the way
from here to morning? I touch
you, made of such nerve
and flare and pride and swallowed tears.
Go home. Come to bed. The skies
look in at us, stern.
And this is an old story.

I dreamed about the war.
We were all sitting at table
in a kitchen in Chicago.
The radio had just screamed
that Illinois was the target.
No one felt like leaving,
we sat by the open window
and talked in the sunset.

I'll tell you that joke tomorrow,
you said with your saddest smile,
if I can remember.

The end is just a straw,
a feather furling slowly down,
floating to light by chance, a breath
on the long-loaded scales.
Posterity trembles like a leaf
and we go on making heirs and heirlooms.
The world, we have to make it,
my coexistent friend said, leaning
back in his cell.
Siberia vastly hulks
behind him, which he did not make.

Oh futile tenderness
of touch in a world like this!
how much longer, dear child,
do you think sex will matter?
There might have been a wedding
that never was:
two creatures sprung free
from castiron covenants.
Instead our hands and minds
erotically waver . . .
Lightness is unavailing.

Catalpas wave and spill
their dull strings across this murk of spring.
I ache, brilliantly.
Only where there is language is there world.
In the harp of my hair, compose me
a song. Death's in the air,
we all know that. Still, for an hour,
I'd like to be gay. How could a gay song go?

Why that's your secret, and it shall be mine.
We are our words, and black and bruised and blue.
Under our skins, we're laughing.

In triste veritas?
Take hold, sweet hands, come on . . .
Broken!
When you falter, all eludes.
This is a seasick way,
this almost/never touching, this
drawing-off, this to-and-fro.
Subtlety stalks in your eyes,
your tongue knows what it knows.
I want your secrets— I *will* have them out.
Seasick, I drop into the sea.

1966

JERUSALEM

In my dream, children
are stoning other children
with blackened carob-pods
I dream my son is riding
on an old grey mare
to a half-dead war
on a dead-grey road
through the cactus and thistles
and dried brook beds.

In my dream, children
are swaddled in smoke
and their uncut hair smolders
even here, here
where trees have no shade
and rocks have no shadow
trees have no memories
only the stones and
the hairs of the head.

I dream his hair is growing
and has never been shorn
from slender temples hanging
like curls of barbed wire
and his first beard is growing
smoldering like fire
his beard is smoke and fire
and I dream him riding
patiently to the war.

What I dream of the city
is how hard it is to leave
and how useless to walk

outside the blasted walls
picking up the shells
from a half-dead war
and I wake up in tears
and hear the sirens screaming
and the carob-tree is bare.

Balfour Street, July 1966

CHARLESTON IN THE 1860's

Derived from the diaries of Mary Boykin Chesnut.

He seized me by the waist and kissed my throat . . .
Your eyes, dear, are they grey or blue,
eyes of an angel?
The carts have passed already with their heaped
night-soil, we breathe again . . .
Is this what war is? Nitrate . . .
But smell the pear,
the jasmine, the violets.
Why does this landscape always sadden you?
Now the freshet is up on every side,
the river comes to our doors,
limbs of primeval trees dip in the swamp.

So we fool on into the black
cloud ahead of us.
Everything human glitters fever-bright—
the thrill of waking up
out of a stagnant life?
There seems a spell upon
your lovers, —all dead of wounds
or blown to pieces . . . Nitrate!
I'm writing, blind with tears of rage.
In vain. Years, death, depopulation, fears,
bondage—these shall all be borne.
No imagination to forestall woe.

1966

NIGHT WATCH

And now, outside, the walls
of black flint, eyeless.
How pale in sleep you lie.
Love: my love is just a breath
blown on the pane and dissolved.
Everything, even you,
cries silently for help, the web
of the spider is ripped with rain,
the geese fly on into the black cloud.
What can I do for you?
what can I do for you?
Can the touch of a finger mend
what a finger's touch has broken?
Blue-eyed now, yellow-haired,
I stand in my old nightmare
beside the track, while you,
and over and over and always you
plod into the deathcars.
Sometimes you smile at me
and I—I smile back at you.
How sweet the odor of the station-master's roses!
How pure, how poster-like the colors of this dream.

1967

THERE ARE SUCH SPRINGLIKE NIGHTS

From the Yiddish of Kadia Molodowsky.

There are such springlike nights here,
when a blade of grass pushes up through the soil
and the fresh dawn is a green pillow
under the skeleton of a dead horse.
And all the limbs of a woman plead for the ache of birth.
And women come to lie down like sick sheep
by the wells—to heal their bodies,
their faces blackened with yearlong thirst for a child's cry.

There are such springlike nights here
when lightning pierces the black soil with silver knives
and pregnant women approach the white tables of the hospital
with quiet steps
and smile at the unborn child
and perhaps at death.

There are such springlike nights here
when a blade of grass pushes up through the soil.

1968

FOR A RUSSIAN POET

1. *The Winter Dream*

Everywhere, snow is falling. Your bandaged foot
drags across huge cobblestones, bells
hammer in distant squares.
Everything we stood against has conquered
and now we're part
of it all. *Life's the main thing,* I hear you say,
but a fog is spreading between this landmass
and the one your voice
mapped so long for me. All that's visible
is walls, endlessly yellow-grey, where
so many risks were taken, the shredded skies
slowly littering both our continents with
the only justice left, burying
footprints, bells and voices with all deliberate speed.

1967

2. *Summer in the Country*

Now, again, every year for years: the life-and-death talk,
late August, forebodings
under the birches, along the water's edge
and between the typed lines

and evenings, tracing a pattern of absurd hopes
in broken nutshells
                          but this year we both
sit after dark with the radio
unable to read, unable to write

trying the blurred edges of broadcasts

for a little truth, taking a walk before bed
wondering what a man can do, asking that
at the verge of tears in a lightning-flash of loneliness.

3. *The Demonstration*

Natalya Gorbanevskaya
13/3 Novopeschanaya Street
Apartment 34

At noon we sit down quietly on the parapet
and unfurl our banners
                      almost immediately
the sound of police whistles
from all corners of Red Square
                      we sit
quietly and offer no resistance
Is this your little boy

we will relive this over and over

the banners torn from our hands
                      blood flowing
a great jagged torn place
in the silence of complicity

that much at least
we did here

In your flat, drinking tea
waiting for the police
your children asleep while you write
quickly, the letters you want to get off
before tomorrow

I'm a ghost at your table
touching poems in a script I can't read

we'll meet each other later

August 1968

NIGHT IN THE KITCHEN

The refrigerator falls silent.
Then other things are audible:
this dull, sheet-metal mind rattling like stage thunder.
The thickness budging forward in these veins
is surely something other
than blood:
say, molten lava.

You will become a black lace cliff fronting a deadpan sea;
nerves, friable as lightning
ending in burnt pine forests.
You are begun, beginning, your black heart drumming
slowly, triumphantly
inside its pacific cave.

1967

5:30 A. M.

Birds and periodic blood.
Old recapitulations.
The fox, panting, fire-eyed,
gone to earth in my chest.
How beautiful we are,
he and I, with our auburn
pelts, our trails of blood,
our miracle escapes,
our whiplash panic flogging us on
to new miracles!
They've supplied us with pills
for bleeding, pills for panic.
Wash them down the sink.
This is truth, then:
dull needle groping in the spinal fluid,
weak acid in the bottom of the cup,
foreboding, foreboding.
No one tells the truth about truth,
that it's what the fox
sees from his scuffled burrow:
dull-jawed, onrushing
killer, being that
inanely single-minded
will have our skins at last.

1967

THE BREAK

All month eating the heart out,
smothering in a fierce insomnia . . .
First the long, spongy summer, drying
out by fits and starts, till a morning
torn off another calendar
when the wind stiffens, chairs
and tables rouse themselves
in a new, unplanned light
and a word flies like a dry leaf down the hall
at the bang of a door.

Then break, October, speak,
non-existent and damning clarity.
Stare me down, thrust
your tongue against mine, break
day, let me stand up
like a table or a chair
in a cold room with the sun beating in
full on the dusty panes.

1967

TWO POEMS

Adapted from Anna Akhmatova.

1.

There's a secret boundary hidden in the waving grasses:
neither the lover nor the expert sensualist
passes it, though mouths press silently together
and the heart is bursting.

And friends—they too are helpless there,
and so with years of fire and joy,
whole histories of freedom
unburdened by sensual languor.

The crazy ones push on to that frontier
while those who have found it are sick with grief . . .
And now you know
why my heart doesn't beat beneath your hand.

2.

On the terrace, violins played
the most heartbreaking songs.
A sharp, fresh smell of the sea
came from oysters on a dish of ice

He said, *I'm a faithful friend,*
touching my dress.
How far from a caress,
the touch of that hand!

The way you stroke a cat, a bird,
the look you give a shapely bareback rider.
In his calm eyes, only laughter
under the light-gold lashes.

And the violins mourn on
behind drifting smoke:
Thank your stars, you're at last alone
with the man you love.

1966

THE KEY

Through a drain grating, something
        glitters and falters,
                glitters again. A scrap of foil,

a coin, a signal, a message
        from the indistinct
                piercing my indistinctness?

How long I have gone round
        and round, spiritless with foreknown defeat,
                in search of that glitter?

Hours, years maybe. The cry of metal
        on asphalt, on iron, the sudden
                ching of a precious loss,

the clear statement
        of something missing. Over and over
                it stops me in my tracks

like a falling star, only
        this is not the universe's loss
                it is mine. If I were only colder,

nearer death, nearer birth, I might let go
        whatever's so bent on staying lost.
                Why not leave the house

locked, to collapse inward among its weeds,
        the letters to darken and flake
                in the drawer, the car

to grow skeletal, aflame with rust
    in the moonlit lot, and walk
        ever after?

O God I am not spiritless,
    but a spirit can be stunned,
        a battery felt going dead

before the light flickers,
    and I've covered this ground too often
        with this yellow disc

within whose beam all's commonplace
    and whose limits are described
        by the whole night.

1967

PICNIC

Sunday in Inwood Park
                    the picnic eaten
the chicken bones scattered
                    for the fox we'll never see
the children playing in the caves
My death is folded in my pocket
                              like a nylon raincoat
What kind of sunlight is it
                    that leaves the rocks so cold?

1967

POSTCARD

Rodin's Orpheus, floodlit, hacked,
clawing I don't know what
with the huge toes of an animal,
gripping the air
above the mitered floors
of the Musée . . .

This comes in the mail and I wonder
what it is to be cast in bronze
like the sender;
who wouldn't live, thirsty, drifting,
obscure, freaked-out
but with a future
still lapping at the door
and a dream of language
unlived behind the clouds?

Orpheus hurts all over
but his throat hurts worst of all.
You can see it: the two knobs
of bronze pain in his neck,
the paralysis of his floodlit lips.

1967

THE BOOK
FOR RICHARD HOWARD.

You, hiding there in your words
like a disgrace
the cast-off son of a family
whose face is written in theirs
who must not be mentioned
who calls collect three times a year
from obscure towns out-of-state
and whose calls are never accepted
You who had to leave alone
and forgot your shadow hanging under the stairs
let me tell you: I have been in the house
I have spoken to all of them
they will not pronounce your name
they only allude to you
rising and sitting, going or coming,
falling asleep and waking,
giving away in marriage or calling for water
on their deathbeds
their faces look into each other and see
you
when they write at night in their diaries they are writing
to you

1968

ABNEGATION

The red fox, the vixen
dancing in the half-light among the junipers,
wise-looking in a sexy way,
Egyptian-supple in her sharpness—
what does she want
with the dreams of dead vixens,
the apotheosis of Reynard,
the literature of fox-hunting?
Only in her nerves the past
sings, a thrill of self preservation.
I go along down the road
to a house nailed together by Scottish
Covenanters, instinct mortified
in a virgin forest,
and she springs toward her den
every hair on her pelt alive
with tidings of the immaculate present.
They left me a westernness,
a birthright, a redstained, ravelled
afghan of sky.
She has no archives,
no heirlooms, no future
except death
and I could be more
her sister than theirs
who chopped their way across these hills
—a chosen people.

1968

II

LEAFLETS

WOMEN
FOR C.R.G.

My three sisters are sitting
on rocks of black obsidian.
For the first time, in this light, I can see who they are.

My first sister is sewing her costume for the procession.
She is going as the Transparent Lady
and all her nerves will be visible.

My second sister is also sewing,
at the seam over her heart which has never healed entirely.
At last, she hopes, this tightness in her chest will ease.

My third sister is gazing
at a dark-red crust spreading westward far out on the sea.
Her stockings are torn but she is beautiful.

1968

IMPLOSIONS

The world's
not wanton
only wild and wavering

I wanted to choose words that even you
would have to be changed by

Take the word
of my pulse, loving and ordinary
Send out your signals, hoist
your dark scribbled flags
but take
my hand

All wars are useless to the dead

My hands are knotted in the rope
and I cannot sound the bell

My hands are frozen to the switch
and I cannot throw it

The foot is in the wheel

When it's finished and we're lying
in a stubble of blistered flowers
eyes gaping, mouths staring
dusted with crushed arterial blues

I'll have done nothing
even for you?

1968

TO FRANTZ FANON

Born Martinique, 1925; dead Washington D.C.,
1961.

I don't see your head
sunk, listening   to the throats
of the torturers and the tortured

I don't see your eyes
deep in the blackness   of your skull
they look off from me   into the eyes

of rats and haunted policemen.
What I see best is the length
of your fingers
pressing the pencil
into the barred page

of the French child's copybook
with its Cartesian squares   its grilled
trap of holy geometry
where your night-sweats streamed out
in language

and your death
a black streak on a white bed
in L'Enfant's city where
the fever-bush sweats off

its thick
petals   year after year
on the mass grave
of revolt

1968

CONTINUUM

Waking thickheaded by crow's light
I see the suitcase packed
for your early plane; nothing to do
but follow the wristwatch hands
round to the hour. Life is like money
—you said, finishing the brandy from the cracked
plastic bathroom cup last night—
no use except for what you can get with it.
Yet something wants us delivered up
alive, whatever it is,
that causes me to edge the slatted blind
soundlessly up, leaving you
ten minutes' more sleep, while I look
shivering, lucidifying, down
at that street where the poor are already getting started
and that poster streaking the opposite wall
with the blurred face of a singer whose songs
money can't buy nor air contain
someone yet unloved, whose voice
I may never hear, but go on hoping
to hear, tonight, tomorrow, someday,
as I go on hoping to feel
tears of mercy in the of course impersonal rain.

1968

ON EDGES

When the ice starts to shiver
all across the reflecting basin
or water-lily leaves
dissect a simple surface
the word 'drowning' flows through me.
You built a glassy floor
that held me
as I leaned to fish for old
hooks and toothed tin cans,
stems lashing out like ties of
silk dressing-gowns
archangels of lake-light
gripped in mud.

Now you hand me a torn letter.
On my knees, in the ashes, I could never
fit these ripped-up flakes together.
In the taxi I am still piecing
what syllables I can
translating at top speed like a thinking machine
that types out 'useless' as 'monster'
and 'history' as 'lampshade'.
Crossing the bridge I need all my nerve
to trust to the man-made cables.

The blades on that machine
could cut you to ribbons
but its function is humane.
Is this all I can say of these
delicate hooks, scythe-curved intentions
you and I handle? I'd rather

taste blood, yours or mine, flowing
from a sudden slash, than cut all day
with blunt scissors on dotted lines
like the teacher told.

1968

VIOLENCE

No one knows yet
what he is capable of. Thus: if you
(still drawing me, mouth to mouth
toward the door) had pushed
a gun into my hand
would my fingers have burned, or not,
to dry ice on that metal?
if you'd said, leaving
in a pre-dawn thunderstorm
use this when the time comes
would I have blurted my first *no* that night
or, back without you, bundled
the cold bulk into a drawer
in a cocoon of nightgowns
printed with knots of honeysuckle . . .
Still following you as if your body
were a lantern, an angel of radar,
along the untrustworthy park
or down that block where the cops shoot to kill—
could I have dreamed a violence
like that of finding
your burnt-out cigarettes
planted at random, charred
fuses in a blown-up field?

1968

THE OBSERVER

Completely protected on all sides
by volcanoes
a woman, darkhaired, in stained jeans
sleeps in central Africa.
In her dreams, her notebooks, still
private as maiden diaries,
the mountain gorillas move through their life term;
their gentleness survives
observation. Six bands of them
inhabit, with her, the wooded highland.
When I lay me down to sleep
unsheltered by any natural guardians
from the panicky life-cycle of my tribe
I wake in the old cellblock
observing the daily executions,
rehearsing the laws
I cannot subscribe to,
envying the pale gorilla-scented dawn
she wakes into, the stream where she washes her hair,
the camera-flash of her quiet
eye.

1968

NIGHTBREAK

Something broken   Something
I need   By someone
I love   Next year
will I remember what
This anger   unreal
                          yet
has to be gone through
The sun to set
on this anger
                    I go on
head down   into it
The mountain pulsing
Into the oildrum   drops
the ball of fire.

Time is quiet   doesn't break things
or even wound   Things are in danger
from people   The frail clay lamps
of Mesopotamia
row on row under glass
in the ethnological section
little hollows for dried-
up oil   The refugees
with their identical
tales of escape   I don't
collect what I can't use   I need
what can be broken.

In the bed the pieces fly together
and the rifts fill   or else
my body is a list   of wounds
symmetrically placed
a village

blown open   by planes
that did not   finish the job

The enemy has   withdrawn
between raids   become invisible
there are
            no agencies
                        of relief
the darkness becomes utter
Sleep   cracked and flaking
sifts over the shaken   target.

What breaks   is night
not day   The white
scar   splitting
over the east
The crack weeping
Time for the pieces
                        to move
dumbly back
            toward each other.

1968

GABRIEL

There are no angels   yet
here comes an angel   one
with a man's face   young
shut-off ·   the dark
side of the moon   turning to me
and saying: I am the plumed
                         serpent   the beast
                         with fangs of fire   and a gentle
                         heart

But he doesn't say that   His message
drenches his body
he'd want to kill me
for using words to name him

I sit in the bare apartment
reading
words stream past me   poetry
twentieth-century rivers
disturbed surfaces   reflecting clouds
reflecting wrinkled neon
but clogged   and mostly
nothing alive left
in their depths

The angel is barely
speaking   to me
Once in a horn of light
he stood   or someone like him
salutations in gold-leaf
ribboning from his lips

Today again   the hair streams
to his shoulders
the eyes reflect   something
like a lost country   or so I think
but the ribbon has reeled itself
up
    he isn't giving
or taking any shit
We glance miserably
across the room   at each other

It's true   there are moments
closer and closer together
when words stick   in my throat
                    'the art of love'
                    'the art of words'
I get your message Gabriel
just   will you stay looking
straight at me
awhile longer

1968

LEAFLETS

1.

The big star, and that other
lonely on black glass
overgrown with frozen
lesions, endless night
the Coal Sack gaping
black veins of ice on the pane
spelling a word:
                    Insomnia
not manic but ordinary
to start out of sleep
turning off and on
this seasick neon
vision, this
division

the head clears of sweet smoke
and poison gas

life without caution
the only worth living
love for a man
love for a woman
love for the facts
protectless

that self-defense be not
the arm's first motion

memory not only
cards of identity

that I can live half a year
as I have never lived up to this time —

Chekhov coughing up blood almost daily
the steamer edging in toward the penal colony
chained men dozing on deck
five forest fires lighting the island

lifelong that glare, waiting.

2.

Your face
          stretched like a mask
                        begins to tear
as you speak of Che Guevara
Bolivia, Nanterre
I'm too young to be your mother
you're too young to be my brother

your tears are not political
they are real water, burning
as the tears of Telemachus
burned

Over Spanish Harlem the moon
swells up, a fire balloon
fire gnawing the edge
of this crushed-up newspaper

                         now
the bodies come whirling
coal-black, ash-white
out of torn windows
and the death columns blacken

whispering
Who'd choose this life?

We're fighting for a slash of recognition,
a piercing to the pierced heart.
Tell me what you are going through —

but the attention flickers
                and will flicker
a matchflame in poison air
a thread, a hair of light
                sum of all answer
to the *Know that I exist!* of all existing things.

3.

If, says the Dahomeyan devil,
someone has courage to enter the fire
the young man will be restored to life.

If, the girl whispers,
I do not go into the fire
I will not be able to live with my soul.

(Her face calm and dark as amber
under the dyed butterfly turban
her back scarified in ostrich-skin patterns.)

4.

Crusaders' wind glinting
off linked scales of sea
ripping the ghostflags
galloping at the fortress
Acre, bloodcaked, lionhearted
raw vomit curdling in the sun
gray walkers walking

straying with a curbed intentness
in and out the inclosures
the gallows, the photographs
of dead Jewish terrorists, aged 15
their fading faces wide-eyed
and out in the crusading sunlight
gray strayers still straying
dusty paths
the mad who live in the dried-up moat
of the War Museum

what are we coming to
what wants these things of us
who wants them

5.

The strain of being born
    over and over has torn your smile into pieces
Often I have seen it broken
    and then re-membered
and wondered how a beauty
    so anarch, so ungelded
will be cared for in this world.
    I want to hand you this
leaflet streaming with rain or tears
    but the words coming clear
something you might find crushed into your hand
    after passing a barricade
and stuff in your raincoat pocket.
    I want this to reach you
who told me once that poetry is nothing sacred
    no more sacred that is
than other things in your life—
    to answer yes, if life is uncorrupted
no better poetry is wanted.

I want this to be yours
in the sense that if you find and read it
    it will be there in you already
and the leaflet then merely something
    to leave behind, a little leaf
in the drawer of a sublet room.
    What else does it come down to
but handing on scraps of paper
    little figurines or phials
no stronger than the dry clay they are baked in
    yet more than dry clay or paper
because the imagination crouches in them.
    If we needed fire to remind us
that all true images
    were scooped out of the mud
where our bodies curse and flounder
    then perhaps that fire is coming
to sponge away the scribes and time-servers
    and much that you would have loved will be lost as well
before you could handle it and know it
    just as we almost miss each other
in the ill cloud of mistrust, who might have touched
    hands quickly, shared food or given blood
for each other. I am thinking how we can use what we have
    to invent what we need.

Winter–Spring 1968

THE RAFTS

FOR DAVID, MICHAEL AND DAVID.

Down the river, on rafts you came
floating. The three of you
and others I can't remember.
Stuck to your sleeves, twists of
blurred red rag, old bandages, ribbons
of honor.   Your hands dragged me
aboard.
          Then I sprawled
full length on the lashed poles
laughing, drenched, in rags.

The river's rising!
                    they yelled on shore
thru megaphones.
Can't you see
that water's mad, those rafts
are children's toys, that crowd
is heading nowhere?
                    My lips
tasted your lips and foreheads
salty with sweat,
then we were laughing, holding off
the scourge of dead branches
overhanging from shore as your
homemade inventions
                    danced
                            along

1968

III

GHAZALS (HOMAGE TO GHALIB)

7/12/68

FOR SHEILA ROTNER.

The clouds are electric in this university.
The lovers astride the tractor burn fissures through the hay.

When I look at that wall I shall think of you
and of what you did not paint there.

Only the truth makes the pain of lifting a hand worthwhile:
the prism staggering under the blows of the raga.

The vanishing-point is the point where he appears.
Two parallel tracks converge, yet there has been no wreck.

To mutilate privacy with a single foolish syllable
is to throw away the search for the one necessary word.

When you read these lines, think of me
and of what I have not written here.

7/13/68

The ones who camped on the slopes, below the bare summit,
saw differently from us, who breathed thin air and kept walking.

Sleeping back-to-back, man and woman, we were more conscious
than either of us awake and alone in the world.

These words are vapor-trails of a plane that has vanished;
by the time I write them out, they are whispering something else.

Do we still have to feel jealous of our creations?
Once they might have outlived us; in this world, we'll die together.

Don't look for me in the room I have left;
the photograph shows just a white rocking-chair, still rocking.

7/14/68: I

In Central Park we talked of our own cowardice.
How many times a day, in this city, are those words spoken?

The tears of the universe aren't all stars, Danton;
some are satellites of brushed aluminum and stainless steel.

He, who was temporary, has joined eternity;
he has deserted us, gone over to the other side.

In the Theatre of the Dust no actor becomes famous.
In the last scene they all are blown away like dust.

"It may be if I had known them I would have loved them."
You were American, Whitman, and those words are yours.

7/14/68: II

Did you think I was talking about my life?
I was trying to drive a tradition up against the wall.

The field they burned over is greener than all the rest.
You have to watch it, he said, the sparks can travel the roots.

Shot back into this earth's atmosphere
our children's children may photograph these stones.

In the red wash of the darkroom, I see myself clearly;
when the print is developed and handed about, the face is
      nothing to me.

For us the work undoes itself over and over:
the grass grows back, the dust collects, the scar breaks open.

7/16/68: I

Blacked-out on a wagon, part of my life cut out forever—
five green hours and forty violet minutes.

A cold spring slowed our lilacs, till a surf broke
violet/white, tender and sensual, misread it if you dare.

I tell you, truth is, at the moment, here
burning outward through our skins.

Eternity streams through my body:
touch it with your hand and see.

Till the walls of the tunnel cave in
and the black river walks on our faces.

7/16/68: II

When they mow the fields, I see the world reformed
as if by snow, or fire, or physical desire.

First snow. Death of the city. Ghosts in the air.
Your shade among the shadows, interviewing the mist.

The mail came every day, but letters were missing;
by this I knew things were not what they ought to be.

The trees in the long park blurring back
into Olmsted's original dream-work.

The impartial scholar writes me from under house arrest.
I hope you are rotting in hell, Montaigne you bastard.

7/17/68

Armitage of scrapiron for the radiations of a moon.
Flower cast in metal, Picasso-woman, sister.

Two hesitant Luna moths regard each other
with the spots on their wings: fascinated.

To resign *yourself*—what an act of betrayal!
—to throw a runaway spirit back to the dogs.

When the ebb-tide pulls hard enough, we are all starfish.
The moon has her way with us, my companion in crime.

At the Aquarium that day, between the white whale's loneliness
and the groupers' mass promiscuities, only ourselves.

7/23/68

When your sperm enters me, it is altered;
when my thought absorbs yours, a world begins.

If the mind of the teacher is not in love with the mind of the student,
he is simply practicing rape, and deserves at best our pity.

To live outside the law! Or, barely within it,
a twig on boiling waters, enclosed inside a bubble

Our words are jammed in an electronic jungle;
sometimes, though, they rise and wheel croaking above the treetops.

An open window; thick summer night; electric fences trilling.
What are you doing here at the edge of the death-camps, Vivaldi?

7/24/68: I

The sapling springs, the milkweed blooms: obsolete Nature.
In the woods I have a vision of asphalt, blindly lingering.

I hardly know the names of the weeds I love.
I have forgotten the names of so many flowers.

I can't live at the hems of that tradition—
will I last to try the beginning of the next?

Killing is different now: no fingers round the throat.
No one feels the wetness of the blood on his hands.

When we fuck, there too are we remoter
than the fucking bodies of lovers used to be?

How many men have touched me with their eyes
more hotly than they later touched me with their lips.

7/24/68: II

The friend I can trust is the one who will let me have my death.
The rest are actors who want me to stay and further the plot.

At the drive-in movie, above the PanaVision,
beyond the projector beams, you project yourself, great Star.

The eye that used to watch us is dead, but open.
Sometimes I still have a sense of being followed.

How long will we be waiting for the police?
How long must I wonder which of my friends would hide me?

Driving at night I feel the Milky Way
streaming above me like the graph of a cry.

7/26/68: I

Last night you wrote on the wall: Revolution is poetry.
Today you needn't write; the wall has tumbled down.

We were taught to respect the appearance behind the reality.
Our senses were out on parole, under surveillance.

A pair of eyes imprisoned for years inside my skull
is burning its way outward, the headaches are terrible.

I'm walking through a rubble of broken sculpture, stumbling
here on the spine of a friend, there on the hand of a brother.

All those joinings! and yet we fought so hard to be unique.
Neither alone, nor in anyone's arms, will we end up sleeping.

7/26/68: II

A dead mosquito, flattened against a door;
his image could survive our comings and our goings.

LeRoi! Eldridge! listen to us, we are ghosts
condemned to haunt the cities where you want to be at home.

The white children turn black on the negative.
The summer clouds blacken inside the camera-skull.

Every mistake that can be made, we are prepared to make;
anything less would fall short of the reality we're dreaming.

Someone has always been desperate, now it's our turn—
we who were free to weep for Othello and laugh at Caliban.

I have learned to smell a *conservateur* a mile away:
they carry illustrated catalogues of all that there is to lose.

7/26/68: III

So many minds in search of bodies
groping their way among artificial limbs.

Of late they write me how they are getting on:
desertion, desertion, is the story of those pages.

A chewed-up nail, the past, splitting yet growing,
the same and not the same; a nervous habit never shaken.

Those stays of tooled whalebone in the Salem museum—
erotic scrimshaw, practical even in lust.

Whoever thought of inserting a ship in a bottle?
Long weeks without women do this to a man.

8/1/68

The order of the small town on the riverbank,
forever at war with the order of the dark and starlit soul.

Were you free then all along, Jim, free at last,
of everything but the white boy's fantasies?

We pleaded guilty till we saw what rectitude was like:
its washed hands, and dead nerve, and sclerotic eye.

I long ago stopped dreaming of pure justice, your honor—
my crime was to believe we could make cruelty obsolete.

The body has been exhumed from the burnt-out bunker;
the teeth counted, the contents of the stomach told over.

And you, Custer the Squaw-killer, hero of primitive schoolrooms—
where are you buried, what is the condition of your bones?

8/4/68

FOR AIJAZ AHMAD.

If these are letters, they will have to be misread.
If scribblings on a wall, they must tangle with all the others.

Fuck reds   Black Power   Angel loves Rosita
—and a transistor radio answers in Spanish: *Night must fall.*

Prisoners, soldiers, crouching as always, writing,
explaining the unforgivable to a wife, a mother, a lover.

Those faces are blurred and some have turned away
to which I used to address myself so hotly.

How is it, Ghalib, that your grief, resurrected in pieces,
has found its way to this room from your dark house in Delhi?

When they read this poem of mine, they are translators.
Every existence speaks a language of its own.

8/8/68: I

From here on, all of us will be living
like Galileo turning his first tube at the stars.

Obey the little laws and break the great ones
is the preamble to their constitution.

Even to hope is to leap into the unknown,
under the mocking eyes of the way things are.

There's a war on earth, and in the skull, and in the glassy spaces,
between the existing and the non-existing.

I need to live each day through, have them and know them all,
though I can see from here where I'll be standing at the end.

8/8/68: II

FOR A.H.C.

A piece of thread ripped-out from a fierce design,
some weaving figured as magic against oppression.

I'm speaking to you as a woman to a man:
when your blood flows I want to hold you in my arms.

How did we get caught up fighting this forest fire,
we, who were only looking for a still place in the woods?

How frail we are, and yet, dispersed, always returning,
the barnacles they keep scraping from the warship's hull.

The hairs on your breast curl so lightly as you lie there,
while the strong heart goes on pounding in its sleep.

THE WILL
TO CHANGE

(1971)

For David, Pablo and Jacob

What does not change / is the will to change
—Charles Olson, "The Kingfishers"

NOVEMBER 1968

Stripped
you're beginning to float free
up through the smoke of brushfires
and incinerators
the unleafed branches won't hold you
nor the radar aerials

You're what the autumn knew would happen
after the last collapse
of primary color
once the last absolutes were torn to pieces
you could begin

How you broke open, what sheathed you
until this moment
I know nothing about it
my ignorance of you amazes me
now that I watch you
starting to give yourself away
to the wind

1968

STUDY OF HISTORY

Out there.   The mind of the river
as it might be you.

Lights   blotted by unseen hulls
repetitive shapes passing
dull foam crusting the margin
barges sunk below the water-line with silence.
The scow, drudging on.

Lying in the dark, to think of you
and your harsh traffic
gulls pecking your rubbish   natural historians
mourning your lost purity
pleasure cruisers
witlessly careening you

but this
after all
is the narrows and after
all we have never entirely
known what was done to you upstream
what powers trepanned
which of your channels diverted
what rockface leaned to stare
in your upturned
defenseless
face.

1968

PLANETARIUM

Thinking of Caroline Herschel, 1750–1848, astronomer,
sister of William; and others.

A woman in the shape of a monster
a monster in the shape of a woman
the skies are full of them

a woman   'in the snow
among the Clocks and instruments
or measuring the ground with poles'

in her 98 years to discover
8 comets

she whom the moon ruled
like us
levitating into the night sky
riding the polished lenses

Galaxies of women, there
doing penance for impetuousness
ribs chilled
in those spaces   of the mind

An eye,
        'virile, precise and absolutely certain'
        from the mad webs of Uranusborg
                                encountering the NOVA

every impulse of light exploding
from the core
as life flies out of us

Tycho whispering at last
'Let me not seem to have lived in vain'

What we see, we see
and seeing is changing

the light that shrivels a mountain
and leaves a man alive

Heartbeat of the pulsar
heart sweating through my body

The radio impulse
pouring in from Taurus

     I am bombarded yet   I stand

I have been standing all my life in the
direct path of a battery of signals
the most accurately transmitted most
untranslateable language in the universe
I am a galactic cloud so deep   so invo-
luted that a light wave could take 15
years to travel through me   And has
taken   I am an instrument in the shape
of a woman trying to translate pulsations
into images   for the relief of the body
and the reconstruction of the mind.

1968

THE BURNING OF PAPER INSTEAD OF CHILDREN

I was in danger of verbalizing my moral impulses out of existence.
                              —Fr. Daniel Berrigan, on trial in Baltimore

1.

My neighbor, a scientist and art-collector, telephones me in a state of violent emotion. He tells me that my son and his, aged eleven and twelve, have on the last day of school burned a mathematics text-book in the backyard. He has forbidden my son to come to his house for a week, and has forbidden his own son to leave the house during that time. "The burning of a book," he says, "arouses terrible sensations in me, memories of Hitler; there are few things that upset me so much as the idea of burning a book."

Back there: the library, walled
with green Britannicas
Looking again
in Dürer's *Complete Works*
for MELENCOLIA, the baffled woman

the crocodiles in Herodotus
the Book of the Dead
the *Trial of Jeanne d'Arc,* so blue
I think, It is her color

and they take the book away
because I dream of her too often

love and fear in a house
knowledge of the oppressor

I know it hurts to burn

2.

To imagine a time of silence
or few words
a time of chemistry and music

the hollows above your buttocks
traced by my hand
or, *hair is like flesh,* you said

an age of long silence

relief

from this tongue   the slab of limestone
or reinforced concrete
fanatics and traders
dumped on this coast   wildgreen   clayred
that breathed once
in signals of smoke
sweep of the wind

knowledge of the oppressor
this is the oppressor's language

yet I need it to talk to you

3.

"People suffer highly in poverty and it takes dignity and intelligence
to overcome this suffering. Some of the suffering are: a child did not
had dinner last night: a child steal because he did not have money
to buy it: to hear a mother say she do not have money to buy food
for her children and to see a child without cloth it will make tears
in your eyes."

(the fracture of order
the repair of speech
to overcome this suffering)

4.

We lie under the sheet
after making love, speaking
of loneliness
relieved in a book
relived in a book
so on that page
the clot and fissure
of it appears
words of a man
in pain
a naked word
entering the clot
a hand grasping
through bars:

deliverance

What happens between us
has happened for centuries
we know it from literature

still it happens

sexual jealousy
outflung hand
beating bed

dryness of mouth
after panting

there are books that describe all this
and they are useless

You walk into the woods behind a house
there in that country
you find a temple
built eighteen hundred years ago
you enter without knowing
what it is you enter

so it is with us

no one knows what may happen
though the books tell everything

burn the texts   said Artaud

5.

I am composing on the typewriter late at night, thinking of today.
How well we all spoke. A language is a map of our failures. Fred-
erick Douglass wrote an English purer than Milton's. People suffer
highly in poverty. There are methods but we do not use them. Joan,
who could not read, spoke some peasant form of French. Some of
the suffering are: it is hard to tell the truth; this is America; I cannot
touch you now. In America we have only the present tense. I am in
danger. You are in danger. The burning of a book arouses no sen-
sation in me. I know it hurts to burn. There are flames of napalm
in Catonsville, Maryland. I know it hurts to burn. The typewriter
is overheated, my mouth is burning, I cannot touch you and this is
the oppressor's language.

1968

I DREAM I'M THE
DEATH OF ORPHEUS

I am walking rapidly through striations of light and dark thrown
    under an arcade.

I am a woman in the prime of life, with certain powers
and those powers severely limited
by authorities whose faces I rarely see.
I am a woman in the prime of life
driving her dead poet in a black Rolls-Royce
through a landscape of twilight and thorns.
A woman with a certain mission
which if obeyed to the letter will leave her intact.
A woman with the nerves of a panther
a woman with contacts among Hell's Angels
a woman feeling the fullness of her powers
at the precise moment when she must not use them
a woman sworn to lucidity
who sees through the mayhem, the smoky fires
of these underground streets
her dead poet learning to walk backward against the wind
on the wrong side of the mirror

1968

THE BLUE GHAZALS

9/21/68

Violently asleep in the old house.
A clock stays awake all night ticking.

Turning, turning their bruised leaves
the trees stay awake all night in the wood.

Talk to me with your body through my dreams.
Tell me what we are going through.

The walls of the room are muttering,
old trees, old utopians, arguing with the wind.

To float like a dead man in a sea of dreams
and half those dreams being dreamed by someone else.

Fifteen years of sleepwalking with you,
wading against the tide, and with the tide.

9/23/68

One day of equinoctial light after another,
moving ourselves through gauzes and fissures of that light.

Early and late I come and set myself against you,
your phallic fist knocking blindly at my door.

The dew is beaded like mercury on the coarsened grass,
the web of the spider is heavy as if with sweat.

Everything is yielding toward a foregone conclusion,
only we are rash enough to go on changing our lives.

An Ashanti woman tilts the flattened basin on her head
to let the water slide downward: I am that woman and that water.

9/26/68: I

A man, a woman, a city.
The city as object of love.

Anger and filth in the basement.
The furnace stoked and blazing.

A sexual heat on the pavements.
Trees erected like statues.

Eyes at the ends of avenues.
Yellow for hesitation.

I'm tired of walking your streets
he says, unable to leave her.

Air of dust and rising sparks,
the city burning her letters.

9/28/68: II
FOR WALLACE STEVENS.

Ideas of order . . . Sinner of the Florida keys,
you were our poet of revolution all along.

A man isn't what he seems but what he desires:
gaieties of anarchy drumming at the base of the skull.

Would this have left you cold, our scene, its wild parades,
the costumes, banners, incense, flowers, the immense marches?

Disorder is natural, these leaves absently blowing
in the drinking-fountain, filling the statue's crevice.

The use of force in public architecture:
nothing, not even the honeycomb, manifests such control.

9/29/68

FOR LEROI JONES.

Late at night I went walking through your difficult wood,
half-sleepy, half-alert in that thicket of bitter roots.

Who doesn't speak to me, who speaks to me more and more,
but from a face turned off, turned away, a light shut out.

Most of the old lecturers are inaudible or dead.
Prince of the night there are explosions in the hall.

The blackboard scribbled over with dead languages
is falling and killing our children.

Terribly far away I saw your mouth in the wild light:
it seemed to me you were shouting instructions to us all.

12/13/68

They say, if you can tell, clasped tight under the blanket,
the edge of dark from the edge of dawn, your love is a lie.

If I thought of my words as changing minds,
hadn't my mind also to suffer changes?

They measure fever, swab the blisters of the throat,
but the cells of thought go rioting on ignored.

It's the inner ghost that suffers, little spirit
looking out wildly from the clouded pupils.

When will we lie clearheaded in our flesh again
with the cold edge of the night driving us close together?

12/20/68: I

There are days when I seem to have nothing
but these frayed packets, done up with rotting thread.

The shortest day of the year, let it be ours.
Let me give you something: a token for the subway.

(Refuse even
the most beloved old solutions.

That dead man wrote, grief ought to reach the lips.
You must believe I know before you can tell me.

A black run through the tunnelled winter, he and she,
together, touching, yet not side by side.

12/20/68: II

Frost, burning. The city's ill.
We gather like viruses.

The doctors are all on their yachts
watching the beautiful skin-divers.

The peasant mind of the Christian
transfixed on food at the year's turning.

Thinking of marzipan
forget that revolutionary child.

Thought grown senile with sweetness.
You too may visit the Virgins.

In the clear air, hijacked planes
touch down at the forbidden island.

5/4/69

Pain made her conservative.
Where the matches touched her flesh, she wears a scar.

The police arrive at dawn
like death and childbirth.

City of accidents, your true map
is the tangling of all our lifelines.

The moment when a feeling enters the body
is political. This touch is political.

Sometimes I dream we are floating on water
hand-in-hand; and sinking without terror.

PIERROT LE FOU

1.

Suppose you stood facing
a wall
      of photographs
from your unlived life

as you stand looking at these
stills from the unseen film?

Yourself against a wall
curiously stuccoed

Yourself in the doorway
of a kind of watchman's hut

Yourself at a window
signaling to people
you haven't met yet

Yourself in unfamiliar clothes
with the same eyes

2.

On a screen as wide as this, I grope for the titles.
I speak the French language like a schoolgirl of the 'forties.
Those roads remind me of Beauce and the motorcycle.
We rode from Paris to Chartres in the March wind.
He said we should go to Spain but the wind defeated me.
France of the superhighways, I never knew you.
How much the body took in those days, and could take!
A naked lightbulb still simmers in my eyeballs.
In every hotel, I lived on the top floor.

3.

Suppose we had time
and no money
living by our wits
                    telling stories

which stories would you tell?

I would tell the story
of Pierrot Le Fou
who trusted
            not a woman
                        but love itself

till his head blew off
not quite intentionally

I would tell all the stories I knew
in which people went wrong
but the nervous system

was right all along

4.

The island blistered our feet.
At first we mispronounced each others' names.
All the leaves of the tree were scribbled with words.
There was a language there but no-one to speak it.
Sometimes each of us was alone.
At noon on the beach our shadows left us.
The net we twisted from memory kept on breaking.
The damaged canoe lay on the beach like a dead animal.
You started keeping a journal on a coconut shell.

5.

When I close my eyes
other films
          have been there all along

a market shot:
bins of turnips, feet
of dead chickens
close-up: a black old woman
buying voodoo medicines

a figure of terrible faith
and I know her needs

Another film:
               an empty room stacked with old films
I am kneeling on the floor
it is getting dark
               they want to close the building
and I still haven't found you

Scanning reel after reel
tundras in negative,
the Bowery
          all those scenes
but the light is failing
                    and you are missing
from the footage of the march
the railway disaster
. the snowbound village

even the shots of the island
miss you
          yet you were there

6.

To record
in order to see

if you know how the story ends
why tell it

To record
in order to forget

the surface is always lucid
my shadows are under the skin

To record
in order to control

the eye of the camera
doesn't weep tears of blood

To record
for that is what one does

climbing your stairs, over and over
I memorized the bare walls

This is my way of coming back

1969

LETTERS: MARCH 1969

1.

Foreknown. The victor
sees the disaster through and through.
His soles grind rocksalt
from roads of the resistance.
He shoulders through rows
of armored faces
he might have loved and lived among.
The victory carried like a corpse
from town to town
begins to crawl in the casket.
The summer swindled on
from town to town, our train
stopping and broiling on the rails
long enough to let on who we were.
The disaster sat up with us all night
drinking bottled water, eating fruit,
talking of the conditions that prevailed.
Outside along the railroad cut
they were singing for our death.

2.

Hopes sparkle like water in the clean carafe.
How little it takes
to restore composure.
White napkins, a tray
of napoleons and cherry tarts
compliments of the airline
which has flown us out of danger.

They are torturing the journalist we drank with
last night in the lounge
but we can't be sure of that
here overlooking the runway
three hours and twenty minutes into another life.
If this is done for us
(and this is done for us)
if we are well men wearing bandages
for disguise
if we can choose our scene
stay out of earshot
break the roll and pour
from the clean carafe
if we can desert like soldiers
abjure like thieves
we may well purchase new virtues at the gate
of the other world.

3.

"I am up at sunrise
collecting data.
The reservoir burns green.
Darling, the knives they have on this block alone
would amaze you.
When they ask my profession I say
I'm a student of weapons systems.
The notes I'm putting together are purely
of sentimental value
my briefcase is I swear useless
to foreign powers, to the police
I am not given I say
to revealing my sources
to handing round copies
of my dossier for perusal.
The vulnerable go unarmed.

I myself walk the floor
a ruinously expensive Swiss hunter's knife
exposed in my brain
eight blades, each one for a distinct purpose,
laid open as on the desk
of an importer or a fence."

4.

Six months back
send carbons you said
but this winter's dashed off in pencil
torn off the pad too fast
for those skills. In the dawn taxi
in the kitchen
burning the succotash
the more I love my life the more
I love you. In a time
of fear. In a city
of fears. In a life
without vacations the paisley fades
winter and summer in the sun
but the best time is now.

My sick friend writes: *what's love?*
This life is nothing, Adrienne!

Her hands bled onto the sill.
She had that trick of reaching outward,
the pane was smashed but only
the calvinist northwind
spat in from the sea.
She's a shot hero. A dying poet.
Even now, if we went for her—
but they've gone with rags and putty to fix the pane.
She stays in with her mirrors and anger.

I tear up answers
I once gave, postcards
from riot and famine go up on the walls
valentines stuck in the mirror
flame and curl, loyalties dwindle
the bleak light dries our tears
without relief. I keep coming back to you

in my head, but you couldn't know that, and
I have no carbons. Prince of pity,
what eats out of your hand?
the rodent pain, electric
with exhaustion, mazed and shaken?
I'd have sucked the wound in your hand to sleep
but my lips were trembling.
Tell me how to bear myself,
how it's done, the light kiss falling
accurately
on the cracked palm.

1969

PIECES

1. *Breakpoint*

The music of words
received as fact

The steps that wouldn't hold us both
splintering in air

The self withheld in an urn
like ashes

To have loved you better than you loved yourself
—whoever you were, to have loved you—

And still to love but simply
as one of those faces on the street

2. *Relevance*

That erudition
how to confront it

The critics wrote answers
the questions were ours

A breast, a shoulder
chilled at waking

The cup of yoghurt
eaten at noon
and no explanations

The books we borrowed
trying to read each other's minds

Paperbacks piling
on both sides of the fireplace
and piled beside the bed

What difference could it make
that those books came
out of unintelligible pain

as daylight out of the hours

when that light burned
atop the insurance tower
all night like the moon

3. *Memory*

Plugged-in to her body
he came the whole way
but it makes no difference

If not this then what
would fuse a connection

(All that burning intelligence about love
what can it matter

Falling in love on words
and ending in silence
with its double-meanings

Always falling and ending
because this world gives no room
to be what we dreamt of being

Are we, as he said
of the generation that forgets
the lightning-flash, the air-raid

and each other

4. *Time and Place*

Liquid mist burning off
along the highway

Slap of water
Light on shack boards

Hauling of garbage
early in the wet street

Always the same, wherever waking,
the old positions
assumed by the mind

and the new day forms
like a china cup

hard, cream-colored, unbreakable
even in our travels

5. *Revelation*

This morning: read Simone Weil
on the loss of grace

drank a glass of water

remembered the dream that woke me:

some one, some more than one
battering into my room
intent to kill me

I crying your name
its two syllables
ringing through sleep

knowing it vain
knowing
you slept unhearing

crying your name
like a spell

like signs executed

by the superstitious

who are the faithful of this world

1969

OUR WHOLE LIFE

Our whole life a translation
the permissible fibs

and now a knot of lies
eating at itself to get undone

Words bitten thru words

meanings burnt-off like paint
under the blowtorch

All those dead letters
rendered into the oppressor's language

Trying to tell the doctor where it hurts
like the Algerian
who has walked from his village, burning

his whole body a cloud of pain
and there are no words for this

except himself

1969

YOUR LETTER

                                        blinds me
like the light of that surf
you thrust your body in
for punishment

or the river of fiery fenders
and windshields
you pour yourself into
driving north to S.F.
on that coast of chrome and oil

I watch for any signal
the tremor of courage
in the seismograph

a flash
where I thought the glare
was steady, smogged & tame

1969

STAND UP

Stand up in my nightgown at the window
almost naked behind black glass

Off from the line of trees the road
beaten, bare, we walked

in the light of the bare, beaten moon.
Almost, you spoke to me. The road

swings past swampground
the soft spots of the earth

you might sink through into location
where their cameras are set up

the underground film-makers waiting to make their film
waiting for you

their cameras pivot toward your head and the film burns
but you're not talking

If I am there you have forgotten my name
you think perhaps 'a woman'

and you drift on, drifter, through the frames
of the movie they are making of this time.

A whole soundtrack of your silence
a whole film

of dark nights and darker rooms
and blank sheets of paper, bare . . .

1969

THE STELAE

FOR ARNOLD RICH

Last night I met you in my sister's house
risen from the dead
showing me your collection

You are almost at the point of giving things away

It's the stelae on the walls I want
that I never saw before

You offer other objects
I have seen time and time again

I think you think you are giving me
something precious

The stelae are so unlike you
swart, indifferent, incised with signs
you have never deciphered

I never knew you had them
I wonder if you are giving them away

1969

SNOW

when it comes down turning
itself in clusters before the flat
light of the shortest day

you see how all turns away
from us how we turn
into our shadows you can see
how we are tested

the individual crystal on the
black skirt of the maxi-coat
under the lens

was it a whole day or just a lifetime
spent studying crystals

on the fire escape while the 'Sixties
were running out
could you see

how the black ladder spun away from us
into whiteness
how over and over
a star became a tear

if no two are alike
then what are we doing
with these diagrams of loss

1969

THE WILL TO CHANGE

1.

FOR L.D., DEAD 11/69.

That Chinese restaurant was a joke
with its repeating fountains

& chopsticks in tissue paper
The vodka was too sweet

the beancurd too hot
You came with your Egyptian hieroglyph

your angel's smile
Almost the next day

as surely as if shot
you were thin air

At the risk of appearing ridiculous—
we take back this halfworld for you

and all whose murders accrue
past your death

2.

FOR SANDRA LEVINSON.

Knocked down in the canefield
by a clumsily swung machete

she is helped to her feet
by Fidel

and snapped by photographers
the blonde Yanqui in jeans

We're living through a time
that needs to be lived through us

(and in the morning papers
Bobby Seale, chalked

by the courtroom artist
defaced by the gag)

3.
FOR D.J.L.

Beardless again, phoning
from a storefront in Yorkville

. . . we need a typewriter, a crib
& Michael's number . . .

I swim to you thru dead
latitudes of fever

. . . accepting the discipline . . .
You mean your old freedom

to disappear—you miss that?
. . . but I can dig having lost it . . .

David, I could dig losing everything.
Knowing what you mean, to make that leap

bite into the fear, over & over
& survive. Hoarding my 'liberty'

like a compulsive—more
than I can use up in a lifetime—

two dozen oranges in the refrigerator
for one American weekend

4.

FOR A.H.C.

At the wings of the mirror, peacock plumes
from the Feast of San Gennaro

gaze thru the dark
All night the A-train forages

under our bedroom
All night I dream of a man

black, gagged, shackled, coffined
in a courtroom where I am

passive, white & silent
though my mouth is free

All night I see his eyes
iridescent under torture

and hear the shuddering of the earth
as the trains tear us apart

5.

The cabdriver from the Bronx
screaming: 'This city's GOTTA die!'

dynamiting it hourly from his soul
as surely as any terrorist

Burning the bodies of the scum on welfare
ejaculating into the flames

(*and,* said Freud,
who welcomed it when it was done?)

the professors of the fact
that someone has suffered

seeking truth in a mist of librium
the artists talking of freedom

in their chains

1969–1970

THE PHOTOGRAPH OF THE UNMADE BED

Cruelty is rarely conscious
One slip of the tongue

one exposure
among so many

a thrust in the dark
to see if there's pain there

I never asked you to explain
that act of violence

what dazed me was our ignorance
of our will to hurt each other

                              .   .   .   .

                    In a flash I understand
                    how poems are unlike photographs

                    (the one saying   This could be
                    the other   This was

                    The image
                    isn't responsible

                    for our uses of it
                    It is intentionless

                    A long strand of dark hair
                    in the washbasin

                    is innocent and yet
                    such things have done harm

.   .   .   .   .   .

These snapshots taken by ghetto children
given for Christmas

Objects blurring into perceptions
No 'art,' only the faults

of the film, the faults of the time
Did mere indifference blister

these panes, eat these walls,
shrivel and scrub these trees—

mere indifference? I tell you
cruelty is rarely conscious

the done and the undone blur
into one photograph of failure

.   .   .   .   .   .

This crust of bread we try to share
this name traced on a window

this word I paste together
like a child fumbling

with paste and scissors
this writing in the sky with smoke

this silence

this lettering chalked on the ruins
this alphabet of the dumb

this feather held to lips
that still breathe and are warm

1969

IMAGES FOR GODARD

1.

Language as city:: Wittgenstein
Driving to the limits
of the city of words

the superhighway streams
like a comic strip

to newer suburbs
casements of shockproof glass

where no one yet looks out
or toward the coast where even now

the squatters in their shacks
await eviction

When all conversation
becomes an interview
under duress

when we come to the limits
of the city

my face must have a meaning

2.

To know the extremes of light
I sit in this darkness

To see the present flashing
in a rearview mirror

blued in a plateglass pane
reddened in the reflection

of the red Triomphe
parked at the edge of the sea

the sea glittering in the sun
the swirls of nebula

in the espresso cup
raindrops, neon spectra

on a vinyl raincoat

3.

To love, to move perpetually
as the body changes

a dozen times a day
the temperature of the skin

the feeling of rise & fall
deadweight & buoyancy

the eye sunk inward
the eye bleeding with speech

('for that moment at least
I wás you—')

To be stopped, to shoot the same scene
over & over

4.

At the end of *Alphaville*
she says *I love you*

and the film begins
that you've said you'd never make

because it's impossible
'things as difficult to show

as horror & war & sickness are'

meaning: love,
to speak in the mouth

to touch the breast
for a woman

to know the sex of a man
That film begins here

yet you don't show it
we leave the theatre

suffering from that

5.

Interior monologue of the poet:
the notes for the poem are the only poem

the mind collecting, devouring
all these destructibles

the unmade studio couch the air
shifting the abalone shells

the mind of the poet is the only poem
the poet is at the movies

dreaming the film-maker's dream but differently
free in the dark as if asleep

free in the dusty beam of the projector
the mind of the poet is changing

the moment of change is the only poem

1970

A VALEDICTION
FORBIDDING MOURNING

My swirling wants. Your frozen lips.
The grammar turned and attacked me.
Themes, written under duress.
Emptiness of the notations.

They gave me a drug that slowed the healing of wounds.

I want you to see this before I leave:
the experience of repetition as death
the failure of criticism to locate the pain
the poster in the bus that said:
my bleeding is under control.

A red plant in a cemetery of plastic wreaths.

A last attempt: the language is a dialect called metaphor.
These images go unglossed: hair, glacier, flashlight.
When I think of a landscape I am thinking of a time.
When I talk of taking a trip I mean forever.
I could say: those mountains have a meaning
but further than that I could not say.

To do something very common, in my own way.

1970

SHOOTING SCRIPT
PART I: 11/69–2/70

1.

We were bound on the wheel of an endless conversation.

Inside this shell, a tide waiting for someone to enter.

A monologue waiting for you to interrupt it.

A man wading into the surf. The dialogue of the rock with the breaker.

The wave changed instantly by the rock; the rock changed by the wave returning over and over.

The dialogue that lasts all night or a whole lifetime.

A conversation of sounds melting constantly into rhythms.

A shell waiting for you to listen.

A tide that ebbs and flows against a deserted continent.

A cycle whose rhythm begins to change the meanings of words.

A wheel of blinding waves of light, the spokes pulsing out from where we hang together in the turning of an endless conversation.

The meaning that searches for its word like a hermit crab.

A monologue that waits for one listener.

An ear filled with one sound only.

A shell penetrated by meaning.

2. *Ghazal V*

Adapted from Mirza Ghalib.

Even when I thought I prayed, I was talking to myself; when I found the door shut, I simply walked away.

We all accept Your claim to be unique; the stone lips, the carved limbs, were never your true portrait.

Grief held back from the lips wears at the heart; the drop that refused to join the river dried up in the dust.

Now tell me your story till the blood drips from your lashes. Any other version belongs to your folklore, or ours.

To see the Tigris in a water-drop . . . Either you were playing games with me, or you never cared to learn the structure of my language.

3.

The old blanket. The crumbs of rubbed wool turning up.

Where we lay and breakfasted. The stains of tea. The squares
of winter light projected on the wool.

You, sleeping with closed windows. I, sleeping in the silver
nitrate burn of zero air.

Where it can snow, I'm at home; the crystals accumulating spell
out my story.

The cold encrustation thickening on the ledge.

The arrow-headed facts, accumulating, till a whole city is
taken over.

Midwinter and the loss of love, going comes before gone, over
and over the point is missed and still the blind will turns for
its target.

4.

In my imagination I was the pivot of a fresh beginning.

In rafts they came over the sea; on the island they put up those stones by methods we can only guess at.

If the vegetation grows as thick as this, how can we see what they were seeing?

It is all being made clear, with bulldozers, at Angkor Wat.

The verdure was a false mystery; the baring of the stones is no solution for us now.

Defoliation progresses; concrete is poured, sheets of glass hauled overland in huge trucks and at great cost.

Here we never travailed, never took off our shoes to walk the final mile.

Come and look into this cellar-hole; this is the foundling of the woods.

Humans lived here once; it became sacred only when they went away.

5.

Of simple choice they are the villagers; their clothes come with them like red clay roads they have been walking.

The sole of the foot is a map, the palm of the hand a letter, learned by heart and worn close to the body.

They seemed strange to me, till I began to recall their dialect.

Poking the spade into the dry loam, listening for the tick of broken pottery, hoarding the brown and black bits in a dented can.

Evenings, at the table, turning the findings out, pushing them around with a finger, beginning to dream of fitting them together.

Hiding all this work from them, although they might have helped me.

Going up at night, hiding the tin can in a closet, where the linoleum lies in shatters on a back shelf.

Sleeping to dream of the unformed, the veil of water pouring over the wet clay, the rhythms of choice, the lost methods.

6.

You are beside me like a wall; I touch you with my fingers and keep moving through the bad light.

At this time of year when faces turn aside, it is amazing that your eyes are to be met.

A bad light is one like this, that flickers and diffuses itself along the edge of a frontier.

No, I don't invest you with anything; I am counting on your weakness as much as on your strength.

This light eats away at the clarities I had fixed on; it moves up like a rodent at the edge of the raked paths.

Your clarities may not reach me; but your attention will.

It is to know that I too have no mythic powers; it is to see the liability of all my treasures.

You will have to see all this for a long time alone.

You are beside me like a wall; I touch you with my fingers and keep trying to move through the bad light.

7.

Picking the wax to crumbs in the iron lip of the candelabrum.

Fingering down the thread of the maze where the green strand cuts across the violet strand.

Picking apart the strands of pain; a warp of wool dipped in burning wax.

When the flame shrinks to a blue bead, there is danger; the change of light in a flickering situation.

Stretched on the loom the light expands; the smell of a smell of burning.

When the change leaves you dark, when the wax cools in the socket, when I thought I prayed, when I was talking to myself under the cover of my darkness.

Someone who never said, "What do you feel?" someone who sat across from me, taking the crumbs of wax as I picked them apart and handed them over.

PART II: 3–7/70

8.

FOR HUGH SEIDMAN.

A woman waking behind grimed blinds slatted across a courtyard she never looks into.

Thinking of the force of a waterfall, the slash of cold air from the thickest water of the falls, slicing the green and ochre afternoon in which he turns his head and walks away.

Thinking of that place as an existence.

A woman reaching for the glass of water left all night on the bureau, the half-done poem, the immediate relief.

Entering the poem as a method of leaving the room.

Entering the paper airplane of the poem, which somewhere before its destination starts curling into ash and comes apart.

The woman is too heavy for the poem, she is a swollenness, a foot, an arm, gone asleep, grown absurd and out of bounds.

Rooted to memory like a wedge in a block of wood; she takes the pressure of her thought but cannot resist it.

You call this a poetry of false problems, the shotgun wedding of the mind, the subversion of choice by language.

Instead of the alternative: to pull the sooty strings to set the window bare to purge the room with light to feel the sun breaking in on the courtyard and the steamheat smothering in the shut-off pipes.

To feel existence as this time, this place, the pathos and force of the lumps of snow gritted and melting in the unloved corners of the courtyard.

9. (Newsreel)

This would not be the war we fought in. See, the foliage is heavier, there were no hills of that size there.

But I find it impossible not to look for actual persons known to me and not seen since; impossible not to look for myself.

The scenery angers me, I know there is something wrong, the sun is too high, the grass too trampled, the peasants' faces too broad, and the main square of the capital had no arcades like those.

Yet the dead look right, and the roofs of the huts, and the crashed fuselage burning among the ferns.

But this is not the war I came to see, buying my ticket, stumbling through the darkness, finding my place among the sleepers and masturbators in the dark.

I thought of seeing the General who cursed us, whose name they gave to an expressway; I wanted to see the faces of the dead when they were living.

Once I know they filmed us, back at the camp behind the lines, taking showers under the trees and showing pictures of our girls.

Somewhere there is a film of the war we fought in, and it must contain the flares, the souvenirs, the shadows of the netted brush, the standing in line of the innocent, the hills that were not of this size.

Somewhere my body goes taut under the deluge, somewhere I am naked behind the lines, washing my body in the water of that war.

Someone has that war stored up in metal canisters, a memory he cannot use, somewhere my innocence is proven with my guilt, but this would not be the war I fought in.

10.

FOR VALERIE GLAUBER.

They come to you with their descriptions of your soul.

They come and drop their mementoes at the foot of your bed; their feathers, ferns, fans, grasses from the western mountains.

They wait for you to unfold for them like a paper flower, a secret springing open in a glass of water.

They believe your future has a history and that it is themselves.

They have family trees to plant for you, photographs of dead children, old bracelets and rings they want to fasten onto you.

And, in spite of this, you live alone.

Your secret hangs in the open like Poe's purloined letter; their longing and their methods will never let them find it.

Your secret cries out in the dark and hushes; when they start out of sleep they think you are innocent.

You hang among them like the icon in a Russian play; living your own intenser life behind the lamp they light in front of you.

You are spilt here like mercury on a marble counter, liquefying into many globes, each silvered like a planet caught in a lens.

You are a mirror lost in a brook, an eye reflecting a torrent of reflections.

You are a letter written, folded, burnt to ash, and mailed in an envelope to another continent.

11.

The mare's skeleton in the clearing: another sign of life.

When you pull the embedded bones up from the soil, the flies collect again.

The pelvis, the open archway, staring at me like an eye.

In the desert these bones would be burnt white; a green bloom grows on them in the woods.

Did she break her leg or die of poison?

What was it like when the scavengers came?

So many questions unanswered, yet the statement is here and clear.

With what joy you handled the skull, set back the teeth spilt in the grass, hinged back the jaw on the jaw.

With what joy we left the woods, swinging our sticks, miming the speech of noble savages, of the fathers of our country, bursting into the full sun of the uncut field.

12.

I was looking for a way out of a lifetime's consolations.

We walked in the wholesale district: closed warehouses, windows, steeped in sun.

I said: those cloths are very old. You said: they have lain in that window a long time.

When the skeletons of the projects shut off the sunset, when the sense of the Hudson leaves us, when only by loss of light in the east do I know that I am living in the west.

When I give up being paraphrased, when I let go, when the beautiful solutions in their crystal flasks have dried up in the sun, when the lightbulb bursts on lighting, when the dead bulb rattles like a seed-pod.

Those cloths are very old, they are mummies' cloths, they have lain in graves, they were not intended to be sold, the tragedy of this mistake will soon be clear.

Vacillant needles of Manhattan, describing hour & weather; buying these descriptions at the cost of missing every other point.

13.

We are driven to odd attempts; once it would not have occurred to me to put out in a boat, not on a night like this.

Still, it was an instrument, and I had pledged myself to try any instrument that came my way. Never to refuse one from conviction of incompetence.

A long time I was simply learning to handle the skiff; I had no special training and my own training was against me.

I had always heard that darkness and water were a threat.

In spite of this, darkness and water helped me to arrive here.

I watched the lights on the shore I had left for a long time; each one, it seemed to me, was a light I might have lit, in the old days.

14.

Whatever it was: the grains of the glacier caked in the boot-cleats;
ashes spilled on white formica.

The death-col viewed through power-glasses; the cube of ice
melting on stainless steel.

Whatever it was, the image that stopped you, the one on which you
came to grief, projecting it over & over on empty walls.

Now to give up the temptations of the projector; to see instead the
web of cracks filtering across the plaster.

To read there the map of the future, the roads radiating from the
initial split, the filaments thrown out from that impasse.

To reread the instructions on your palm; to find there how the
lifeline, broken, keeps its direction.

To read the etched rays of the bullet-hole left years ago in the
glass; to know in every distortion of the light what fracture is.

To put the prism in your pocket, the thin glass lens, the map
of the inner city, the little book with gridded pages.

To pull yourself up by your own roots; to eat the last meal in
your old neighborhood.

POEMS

(1969)

THE DAYS: SPRING

He writes: *Let us bear*
our illusions together . . .
I persist in thinking:
every fantasy I have
comes true; who am I
to bear illusions?

He writes: *But who can be*
a saint?—The woman in #9
is locked in the bathroom.
She screams for five hours,
pounds the walls, hears voices
retreating in the hall.
The lock is broken.
The lovers pass and go out to lunch,
boredom sets in by 2 o'clock.

Emptiness of the mirror, and
the failure of the classics.
A look at the ceiling
in pauses of lovemaking:
that immense, scarred domain.

He writes: *The depth of pain*
grows all the time.
We marched and sat down in the street,
she offered her torn newspaper.
Who will survive Amerika?
they sang on Lenox Avenue.

This early summer weekend.
The chance of beginning again.
From always fewer chances

the future plots itself.
I walk Third Avenue,
bare-armed with flowing hair.
Later the stars come out like facts,
my constellation streams at my head,
a woman's body nailed with stars.

1969

TEAR GAS

October 12, 1969: reports of the tear-gassing of demonstrators protesting the treatment of G.I. prisoners in the stockade at Fort Dix, New Jersey.

This is how it feels to do something you are afraid of.
That they are afraid of.

> (Would it have been different at Fort Dix, beginning
> to feel the full volume of tears in you, the measure
> of all you have in you to shed, all you have held
> back from false pride, false indifference, false
> courage

> beginning to weep as you weep peeling onions, but
> endlessly, for the rest of time, tears of chemistry,
> tears of catalyst, tears of rage, tears for yourself,
> tears for the tortured men in the stockade and for
> their torturers

> tears of fear, of the child stepping into the adult
> field of force, the woman stepping into the male field
> of violence, tears of relief, that your body was here,
> you had done it, every last refusal was over)

Here in this house my tears are running wild
in this Vermont of india-madras-colored leaves, of cesspool-
   stricken brooks, of violence licking at old people and
   children
and I am afraid
of the language in my head
I am alone, alone with language
and without meaning
coming back to something written years ago:
our words misunderstand us

wanting a word that will shed itself like a tear
onto the page
leaving its stain

Trying every key in the bunch to get the door even ajar
not knowing whether it's locked or simply jammed from long disuse
trying the keys over and over then throwing the bunch away
staring around for an axe
wondering if the world can be changed like this
if a life can be changed like this

It wasn't completeness I wanted
(the old ideas of a revolution that could be foretold, and once
        arrived at would give us ourselves and each other)
I stopped listening long ago to their descriptions
of the good society

The will to change begins in the body not in the mind
My politics is in my body, accruing and expanding with every
        act of resistance and each of my failures
Locked in the closet at 4 years old I beat the wall with my body
that act is in me still

No, not completeness:
but I needed a way of saying
(this is what they are afraid of)
that could deal with these fragments
I needed to touch you
with a hand, a body
but also with words
I need a language to hear myself with
to see myself in
a language like pigment released on the board
blood-black, sexual green, reds
veined with contradictions
bursting under pressure from the tube

staining the old grain of the wood
like sperm or tears
but this is not what I mean
these images are not what I mean
(I am afraid.)
I mean that I want you to answer me
when I speak badly
that I love you, that we are in danger
that she wants to have your child, that I want us to have mercy
    on each other
that I want to take her hand
that I see you changing
that it was change I loved in you
when I thought I loved completeness
that things I have said which in a few years will be forgotten
matter more to me than this or any poem
and I want you to listen
when I speak badly
not in poems but in tears
not my best but my worst
that these repetitions are beating their way
toward a place where we can no longer be together
where my body no longer will demonstrate outside your stockade
and wheeling through its blind tears will make for the open air
of another kind of action

(I am afraid.)
It's not the worst way to live.

1969

NOTES

THE DIAMOND CUTTERS

The Tourist and the Town. The pronouns in the third section were origi-
nally masculine. But the tourist was a woman—myself—and I never saw
her as anything else. In 1953, when the poem was written, a notion of
male experience as universal prevailed which made the feminine pronoun
suspect or merely "personal." In this poem, as in "Afterward" (p. 23), I
later altered the pronouns because they alter, for me, the dimensions of
the poem.

Villa Adriana. The summer palace built by the Emperor Hadrian for his
favorite boy lover, Antinoüs. In "Antinoüs: The Diaries" *(Snapshots of a
Daughter-in-Law)* I let the young man speak for me.

The Snow Queen. Hans Christian Andersen's tale was the point of depar-
ture.

The Diamond Cutters. Thirty years later I have trouble with the inform-
ing metaphor of this poem. I was trying, in my twenties, to write about
the craft of poetry. But I was drawing, quite ignorantly, on the long
tradition of domination, according to which the precious resource is yielded
up into the hands of the dominator as if by a natural event. The enforced
and exploited labor of actual Africans in actual diamond mines was invis-
ible to me and, therefore, invisible in the poem, which does not take
responsibility for its own metaphor. I note this here because this kind of
metaphor is still widely accepted, and I still have to struggle against it in
my work. *(1984)*

SNAPSHOTS OF A DAUGHTER-IN-LAW

Snapshots of a Daughter-in-Law, 4. "My Life had stood—a Loaded Gun,"
Emily Dickinson, *Complete Poems,* ed. T. H. Johnson, 1960, p. 369.

Snapshots of a Daughter-in-Law, 7. "To have in this uncertain world some stay," from Mary Wollstonecraft, *Thoughts on the Education of Daughters*, London, 1787.

Snapshots of a Daughter-in-Law, 8. "Vous mourez toutes à quinze ans," from Diderot's *Lettres à Sophie Volland*, quoted by Simone de Beauvoir in *Le Deuxième Sexe*, vol. II, pp. 123–4.

Snapshots of a Daughter-in-Law, 10. Cf. *Le Deuxième Sexe*, vol. II, p. 574: ". . . elle arrive du fond des ages, de Thèbes, de Minos, de Chichen Itza; et elle est aussi le totem planté au coeur de la brousse africaine; c'est un helicoptère et c'est un oiseau; et voilà la plus grande merveille: sous ses cheveux peints le bruissement des feuillages devient une pensée et des paroles s'échappent de ses seins."

Artificial Intelligence. See Herbert Simon, *The New Science of Management Decision*, p. 26. "*A General Problem-Solving Program:* Computer programs have been written that enable computers to discover proofs for theorems in logic or geometry, to play chess, to design motors . . . to compose music. . . . From almost all of them, whether intended as simulations [of human processes] or not, we learn something about human problem solving, thinking, and learning. The first thing we learn . . . is that we can explain these human processes *without* postulating mechanisms at subconscious levels that are different from those that are partly conscious and partly verbalized. . . . The secret of problem solving is that there is no secret."

Always the Same. The last line is quoted from D. H. Lawrence, letter to Henry Savage, in *The Collected Letters of D. H. Lawrence*, ed. Harry T. Moore, vol. I, p. 258.

NECESSITIES OF LIFE

In the Woods. The first line is borrowed and translated from the Dutch poet J. C. Bloem.

"*I Am in Danger—Sir—.*" See Thomas Johnson and Theodora Ward, eds., *The Letters of Emily Dickinson* (Cambridge: Harvard University Press, 1958), vol. II, p. 409.

POEMS 1962–1965

White Night. This poem and "There Are Such Springlike Nights" (p. 299) were adapted from the Yiddish with the aid of transliterated versions and prose translations provided by Eliezer Greenberg and Irving Howe, in whose anthology, *A Treasury of Yiddish Poetry* (New York: Holt, Rinehart and Winston, 1969), these first appeared.

LEAFLETS

Orion. One or two phrases suggested by Gottfried Benn's essay "Artists and Old Age," in *Primal Vision: Selected Writings,* ed. E. B. Ashton (New York: New Directions, 1960).

Dwingelo. The site of an astronomical observatory in Holland.

Charleston in the 1860's. See Ben Ames Williams, ed., *A Diary from Dixie* (Boston: Houghton Mifflin, 1963).

For a Russian Poet, 3. This poem is based on an account by the poet Natalya Gorbanevskaya of a protest action against the Soviet invasion of Czechoslovakia. Gorbanevskaya was later held, and bore a child, in a "penal mental institution" for her political activities.

Two Poems (adapted from Anna Akhmatova). Based on literal prose versions in Dimitri Obolensky, ed., *The Penguin Book of Russian Verse* (London: Penguin, 1962).

To Frantz Fanon. Revolutionary philosopher; studied medicine at the Sorbonne; worked as a psychiatrist in Algeria during the Franco-Algerian war; died of cancer at thirty-six. Author of *The Wretched of the Earth; Toward the African Revolution; Black Skin, White Masks; A Dying Colonialism.*

The Observer. Suggested by a brief newspaper account of the fieldwork of Diane Fossey. She more recently wrote of her observations in *Gorillas in the Mist* (Boston: Houghton Mifflin, 1983).

Leaflets, 2. "The love of a fellow-creature in all its fullness consists simply in the ability to say to him: 'What are you going through?' " (Simone Weil, *Waiting for God*).

Ghazals (Homage to Ghalib). This poem began to be written after I read Aijaz Ahmed's literal English versions of the Urdu poetry of Mirza Ghalib (1797–1869). While the structure and metrics of the classical *ghazal* form used by Ghalib are much stricter than mine, I adhered to his use of a minimum five couplets to a *ghazal,* each couplet being autonomous and independent of the others. The continuity and unity flow from the associations and images playing back and forth among the couplets in any single *ghazal.* The poems are dated as I wrote them, during a month in the summer of 1968. Although I was a contributor to Ahmad's *The Ghazals of Ghalib* (New York: Columbia University Press, 1971), the *ghazals* here are not translations, but original poems.

My *ghazals* are personal and public, American and twentieth-century; but they owe much to the presence of Ghalib in my mind: a poet self-educated and profoundly learned, who owned no property and borrowed his books, writing in an age of political and cultural break-up.

INDEX

Index 429